The 9 – 5 Marathon Man

Stuart Hayden

Copyright © 2012 Stuart Hayden

All rights reserved.

ISBN-13: 978-1468076851

ISBN-10: 146807685X

DEDICATION

I would like to dedicate this book to my wonderful wife Lucy, who has supported me through the many months of training, and for listening to me explain about how important it was to run the New York City Marathon in under four hours and what it would mean to me.

Without this support I would not have been able to dedicate my time to achieve my goal.

1 – London Marathon April 2011	10
2 – Your worst nightmare	15
3 – Sunday 24th April and looking ahead	19
4 – The lifeline	21
5 – Training through the summer	29
6 – Fitness review	33
7 - Race practice: Oxford Half	35
8 –The next few weeks' training	42
9 – Letchworth 10K 2nd October	43
10 – Last few weeks of training	47
11 – Final long run 18 miles	49
12 – My final discovery: hill training	51
13 – My final 2 weeks	54
14 – 1 week to go	57
15 – Overnight at Heathrow	59
16 – 4th Nov Virgin flight VS021 to New York	60
17 – A devastating blow to the trip	61
18 – Arrival at JFK Airport	65
19 – Saturday 5th November 2011	68
20 – The Big Day – Sunday 6th November	76

21 - Final moments before the start	83
22 – The Corrals	86
23 – The race begins at 10:10	89
24 – The final stages – Central Park	101
25 – The finish	104
26 – Celebrations in Greenwich Village	115
27 – Monday 7th November, the day after	118
28 – How did I achieve my goal?	120

Introduction

I wrote this book based on my experiences from April 2011 after my failure to run the London Marathon due to a back injury that I sustained 48 hours beforehand, after having what I thought was a routine relaxing sports massage.

I want to share my experience with other runners to show that if you believe in something strongly enough and set yourself realistic goals then you can achieve it. I also have a demanding day job as an IT technical team leader and found most marathon training books don't take this into account so this was also the reason I wanted to share a more realistic marathon training program with others.
.
My goal has always been to complete the New York City Marathon in less than four hours. This book describes how I achieved my amazing personal goal after only my third marathon.

It starts with my disappointment on missing out on the 2011 London Marathon, describes the pain and anguish I went through on 22nd April, the lifeline I was given on Monday 25th April for another chance to achieve my goal of a sub four-hour New York City Marathon and what I went through to achieve this.

With my back injury, would I ever be able to run again and get back to the exercise I loved? I certainly didn't want to turn into a couch potato for the rest of my life!

Here I share my training plan and tips, the factors I found enhanced my performance, such as my diet and running gear, followed by the most amazing experience of arriving in New York, the hours leading up to the biggest marathon in the world and finally the run itself where I hoped to achieve my dream.

The early stages of the New York City Marathon 2011.

The following are words of encouragement that really describe my feelings & experiences of the New York City Marathon

The New York City Marathon should be on everybody's list of 'things to do before I die'.

Nowadays running a marathon is much more than completing a 26.2 mile course before collapsing in a monstrous heap.

Most people do their bit for charity, raising hundreds, if not thousands of pounds along the way.

Training for a marathon takes over your life. Weekends are no longer for family, leisure or resting.

Saturdays are for races and Sundays are for the dreaded 'long run' (anything between 10 and 23 miles).

But the months of training - the blood, sweat and tears come rain or shine - have their rewards.

And the New York City Marathon is the ultimate prize for the amateur long distance runner.

Iconic is a word that is often used too liberally, but in the Big Apple's most famous race the term is justified.

At mile 21, as your body wilts with tiredness, your legs buckle with a mind of their own and you can no longer recall why you decided to do the damned run in the first place, the Empire State Building comes into view.

The haze of exhaustion clears as you remember that you are close to finishing one of the world's greatest races.

You stride down Fifth Avenue, roared on by a crowd so vocal that you'd be forgiven for thinking they had a sizeable bet on you.

Marcus Garvey Park, at the heart of Harlem, comes and goes in a blink of an eye.

And then you know you are close.

Central Park, the home straight, is just a few paces away.

You enter to a great cheer as crowds five or six deep jostle for a view of the brave men and women battling to drag themselves through the last three miles.

It's tough, each step is a monumental effort and the temptation to stop is almost overwhelming.

And then the signs tell you that you are two hundred metres from the finish.

The crowds stand, you check your time, the emotion hits you - this is what it's all been for.

The elation of finishing is indescribable.

A foil blanket is wrapped around your shoulders, a huge gold medal is hung around your neck and runners of all nationalities congratulate each other on their epic achievement.

On your 42-kilometre journey you have taken in Staten Island, Brooklyn, Queens, the Bronx, and Manhattan.

You have crossed the Verrazano-Narrows Bridge, the Queensboro Bridge, Willis Avenue Bridge and Madison Avenue Bridge.

The Statue of Liberty, Brooklyn Bridge and the Empire State Building are just three of the landmarks you notice on your way.

And then there are the New Yorkers themselves.

Lining the streets from start to finish, there is no let-up when it comes to support.

For those who had the forethought to write their names on their running vests the reward is priceless.

New Yorkers don't just call your name - they bellow it at the top of their voices.

If you read their placards, of which there are thousands, you'll get a personal cheer.

And if you run along the side of the road like I did for looking for some inspiration you will get hundreds of high fives.

Suddenly you feel like you are leading the race and you forget that you are in a pack of 15,000.

Such a huge event, with more than 47,000 runners, can be intimidating.

But New York Road Runners, together with British sports holiday experts <u>Sports Tours International</u>, had thought of everything.

There was no queue at all when we picked up our race numbers and bibs the day before the race in Downtown Manhattan.

Getting to the start line was easy. After being escorted by a <u>Sport Tours International</u> agent on a short walk to the official bus stop, a convoy of buses picked up runners to take us to the start line <u>sixteen miles away in Staten Island</u>.

At the official start area we were corralled into three villages where there was free tea, coffee, water, bagels and assorted nutrition bars.

There were ample toilets and baggage was transported to the finish line for collection.

Most runners left their unwanted layers at the start line, where charity shops picked them up for resale the next day.

At the finish there was a huge medical staff on hand.

Sightseeing in the following days was slow and stiff.

But the knowledge of the achievement, and the memory of the race, helped the pain ease away.

1 – London Marathon April 2011

My marathon journey began on Friday 22nd April 2011. I had booked a day's holiday from work, which I would typically do prior to a marathon to travel into London to the Excel Centre in the Docklands to register and collect my official running number. I entered the marathon through a charity called VICTA, which stands for 'visually impaired children taking action', and get my name printed on my rainbow-coloured vest in order for the crowd to cheer me on when I was on a low, perhaps after eighteen or twenty miles when in previous races I had hit 'the wall'. The charity supports families and children who are blind or visually impaired and enriches their lives by providing them with specialist care and equipment.

I took the half-hour train journey into London Kings Cross from Hitchin, the historic market town where I live. On the train as I stared out the window watching the countryside pass by, my thoughts were all about Sunday, my heart was beating fast in my excitement and anticipation of taking part in the world-renowned London Marathon, my third in as many years.

I had always been active from a young age, playing football and a variety of other sports and as I got older running was something I always enjoyed. It not only helped me to stay fit but to unwind after a stressful day. Something else which contributed to my love of fitness was the five years working in Australia in my early thirties. I always loved and admired the healthy lifestyle there and regularly went running on the beach. It was this outdoors lifestyle again which inspired me to take my running to another level back in October 2008 when I returned back from my honeymoon in California. Similarly to Australians, the Californians had high fitness levels and were regularly running along the beaches and swinging on the monkey bars in 35 degrees of heat. I felt it was time for me to set myself a challenge. I decided to enter the London Marathon and try to achieve what would be the hardest run of my life in less than four hours.

I walked down to the Circle line of the London Underground at Kings Cross station and took an eastbound train to Tower Hill, where I had to change onto the DLR at Tower Gateway for the final leg of the journey to the Excel Centre in the Docklands. I took the next available train from platform two and passed by the famous O2 arena, formerly known as the Millennium Dome. As the doors of the train opened, I could feel the buzz about the place, people smiling, laughing, talking about their predicted times etc and there was a spring in everyone's step. There were all sorts of people: fat, thin, large, small, tall, smart and scruffy, all with their Virgin-sponsored red goodie bags and lots of people already leaving with their cherished running numbers.

As I approached the entrance of the London Marathon Expo, a great friend of mine, Barry, who I've known since I was thirteen, called and offered to sponsor me a hundred pounds to allow me to reach the amazing sponsorship total of two thousand pounds for VICTA. This would beat my previous two years of sponsorship, a personal achievement for me just to give something back to the charity that I was running for. After all, when you put it into perspective, helping others in need is what really matters; running a marathon is secondary to raising money for worthwhile causes. I thanked Barry profusely, and he agreed that he would log onto the website later on that day to make that milestone donation.

Arriving at the registration zones, I found a friendly atmosphere and bright red everywhere I looked. I walked to my running number kiosk, produced my passport and registration form as ID and waited in my line: numbers 48,500-49,500. I was greeted by a very friendly lady who made me feel really special that I was running again, and I received my running number, timing chip and a large red Virgin-sponsored bag loaded with various marketing and advertising leaflets. All around me within the exhibition hall was official London Marathon merchandise, along with a number of other stands such as ASICS, adidas, New Balance, food supplement stalls, running machines, a giant treadmill, stages for guest speakers and lots of freebie stalls for the runners. I took in the vibe of the event and listened to everything around me, feeling relaxed inside despite knowing that Sunday was just around the corner. As I wandered from stall to stall I picked up various race timings, wrist straps, food supplements and more. I watched the famous UK runner Liz Yelling on the main stage with other excited runners on a giant treadmill.

One of the main reasons for attending the expo was to have my name printed on my vest across my chest so that the crowds to spur me on when I hit a tough period. I queued up at the vest printing kiosk, paid my £8 fee and was told by the assistant the vest would be ready for collection in about an hour. The time was now 11:30am. While I waited I decided to wander around the numerous stalls again and ended up at the main stage where a guest speaker was talking about nutrition and what runners should be eating during the race on Sunday. As I turned away from the guest speaker I saw a stand with relaxing sports massage tables sponsored by adidas. I wandered over, hoping to kill a bit more time, and asked the assistant, who was dressed in brilliant white adidas t-shirt and shorts, how long the massage would last and how much it would cost.

I was sure that a fifteen-minute massage would be a good way for me to unwind and relax before Sunday. There were fifteen to twenty massage therapists, all working hard on their customers, all dressed in the brilliant white adidas outfits. There was lots of marathon chat in progress and the smell of the oils was very distinct in the air, while a background murmur of relaxing zen music could be heard coming from somewhere in the massage area.

After five minutes of waiting a friendly grey-haired chap wearing the brilliant white adidas sports attire called me over to the next available massage table. He introduced himself as Alan and asked if I would like to concentrate on any particular area that required extra work ahead of Sunday's race - knees, legs, hip, ankles etc. I replied with: "just a relaxing leg massage that will put me in good shape for Sunday."

During the massage we exchanged marathon stories about predicted times, past experiences and how many marathons each of us had run. He mentioned that he was lucky enough to run the New York City Marathon several years ago and told me it was best to add an extra fifteen minutes to your predicted time due to the amount of steep inclines, bridges and the soul-destroying last two miles in Central Park. It was inspiring to listen to and it got me thinking that perhaps one day I could also run a marathon overseas and even that greatest and largest marathon in NEW YORK! As the massage continued on my lower legs, ankles, knees and thighs, I lay on the bed in silence, dreaming about running through Manhattan. My muscles now felt loose and relaxed and I felt a warm glow about me. I was now in the right frame of mind and any nervous energy I'd previously felt had reduced, leaving me feeling calm and still inside.

During the final few minutes, as I was lying face down on the table, Alan identified a 'tightness' on my left side. He advised on some stretches while pushing my left leg very slowly up and forward so it was pressed against my left buttock. I felt an uncomfortable dull pain, but it also felt relaxing at the same time; a strange combination to be feeling at that moment really.

We exchanged a few final words of encouragement for Sunday and I clambered off the massage table feeling rather oily and sticky, but in a 'chilled' state of mind. I made my way to the vest printing collection point in a bit of a daze; tiredness had just kicked in following my fifteen-minute session. I was hungry, thirsty and tired. I collected my charity vest with my name – STU - emblazoned in big black bold letters across the vest. I placed my vest in my Virgin goodie bag and pulled out a small nutritional breakfast bar and water to combat my sudden tiredness.

My journey back to Hitchin was pretty average, although I felt a distinct lack of energy as I stepped through the front door of our Victorian semi-detached house in leafy Hertfordshire. I sat and reflected my day to this point while relaxing in the garden, sipping on another Lucozade sports drink. I went through my pre-race routine time and time again: race number, shorts, the correct socks, plasters, Vaseline for chafing, trainers (not too tightly laced), sunglasses, kit bag, breakfast bars, race timing straps, Ironman watch... My heart was beating fast while I ran through my mental checklist several times over before I was happy that I had everything in order and under control.

The evening was spent with a visit to the local Italian pasta restaurant, having a healthy pasta dish to top up the glycogen levels to ensure I was in good shape for the race on Sunday, followed by regular intake of water : seven to eight fluid ounces every two hours. I was beginning to feel full all of the time after drinking at such regular intervals, even over-hydrated at times. I retired to my bed at around 10.30pm for a good night's sleep....or so I thought...

2 – Your worst nightmare

The bedroom was warm, the sash windows were open slightly, allowing a warm breeze to drift into our bedroom. It was like a warm summer morning. I became restless and saw every hour on the clock, wishing that I could sleep for several hours without waking up. The sun shone through the venetian blinds at six on Saturday morning. Only one more sleep until the big race. The bedroom was heating up as the outside temperature had risen to 14 degrees by half-past seven. I lay still, going through my routine again for another thirty minutes until I couldn't take any more.

I shuffled to the edge of the bed, moved from my back and brought my right leg over my left side and suddenly felt a sharp shooting pain in my lower left back...AAAAARRRRRGGGGGGGHHHHHHH! The stabbing and sickening pain jagged down the left side of my body. I was in agony and that pain was unbearable. I was stuck, hanging out over the edge of the bed, unable to move any part of my body. My wife Lucy had already left for work so I was stranded and the thought of reaching the start line of the marathon on Sunday sent shudders through my body. Sweat was beading and dripping from my temples...DESPAIR is the only word to describe my state of mind.

I tried moving onto my back to rethink how I should dismount from the bed to become mobile and stand any chance of taking part in the marathon. I tried again to bring my right leg over in a single move, with the pain still shooting through the left of my lower back. I fell onto my knees, doubled over in the worst pain I had ever experienced. I crawled slowly on my knees and into the bathroom to find some painkillers. Hey Presto - I needed some luck right now - the tablets were in the bottom drawer of our vintage white cabinet. I found a kneeling position that was the most comfortable, although still very painful, waiting for the painkillers to take effect before attempting any more body manoeuvres.

Approximately thirty minutes later, I held onto the bathroom sink and clambered onto one knee, then eased myself up onto both feet...AAAARRRRRRGGGGGHHHHH. I managed to stand up tall but the pain was like a belt wrapping my waist really tightly with a sharp knife piercing deep into my lower back. Slowly and surely I slid down each of the thirteen stairs and sat at the bottom of the stairs contemplating my next move. I called Lucy on her mobile and explained what had happened; she was more upset than me, knowing the hard work I had put in over the last four months to compete.

I weighed up my options and decided on a visit to the Oriental health shop in the centre of town for some acupuncture. I rang through and booked an emergency appointment. I dragged myself up the stairs and into the bedroom, pulled on my shorts, t-shirt and a pair of flip flops and after another frustratingly slow and painful descent down the steep Victorian stairs left the house and shuffled slowly down the road into town for a ten o'clock appointment. I had used this method of acupuncture to fix a niggling injury from a previous year and it had allowed me to run the London Marathon in 2010 without any issues. Second time lucky? Everything was crossed.

I opened the door of the Chinese medicine shop, shuffled into the waiting room area, and stood still, explaining my pain and that I had to be running the marathon on Sunday. The Chinese doctor looked puzzled, uneasy in his reply, looking a bit blank as I explained the symptoms. He led me into the treatment room for a thirty-minute session of acupuncture and a heat lamp to reduce the stiffness and allow the muscles to move more freely. I sank my head through the hole in the massage table, and fell asleep thinking that when I woke it would just be a bad dream and that everything would be ok. A door opened and I woke up, the heat lamp clicked off and the doctor removed each needle from my lower back. I felt a light twist and discomfort from the removal of each of the fifteen needles.

My next thought was that I would be cured. I eased myself from the massage table and slowly sat up. The pain had eased a little, but still throbbed dully, only allowing me to move very slowly. I eased myself from the bed and walked towards the doctor and asked him if he thought I would be able to run on Sunday. I did not receive the positive response that I had hoped for. In fact I didn't receive a direct response at all. The only advice I was given was to apply some herbal massage oil to my lower left back every four hours. At this point my slim hope slipped away and disappeared. I would NOT be running in the 2011 London Marathon. No way... I was gutted. Devastated.

I hobbled out of the Chinese doctor's surgery and through the streets, shoulders drooped. I returned home and slumped on the brown velour sofa. My world had ended, well, temporarily. Thoughts in my mind went flashing past as on a conveyor belt; all that training for it to end like this. I lay on the sofa, often moving to adjust my posture in search of the best position and the least amount of pain. I continued to drink the Lucozade sports drinks and eat the breakfast bars, the chicken sandwich and all the other recommended food as if I was still running the marathon. I could only hope that I would suddenly snap out of this nightmare and the world would return to its normal state. I lay on the sofa for another three hours until Lucy returned home to see how I was feeling. I explained my pain and that the Chinese doctor had confirmed that I had a muscle spasm in the lower left back and nothing was going to fix it this late in the day. Not even *Jim'll Fix It* would be able to fix this. I needed a miracle at this stage, I thought to myself, if I was going to stand any chance of running on Sunday. For those that cannot remember the British TV show, *Jim'll Fix It* was a children's show where 'dreams would come true'. Young viewers would write in to make a wish come true, whether it was to meet a famous personality or to go to a very unusual place...

I left it as late as possible - until six in the evening on Saturday - to make my go/no-go decision on my back injury. This was the moment of truth. I called the VICTA charity helpline to explain my situation and received a positive response which explained that as long as I didn't start the race, my place would be deferred and I would have an automatic place for the 2012 London Marathon with the £2000.00 sponsorship money carried over.

Phew...It was seven o'clock and I had officially given up any hope of taking part. I sat staring into space looking for some inspiration, but all I could find was despair. I went to bed on Saturday after dinner feeling so low, yet after all nobody had died and the world wasn't going to end, was it? I just couldn't take part in a marathon; it was only a race. But I felt a kind of heartbreak from getting so near. Would I ever be able to run again? Would I always have a bad back from this moment on? And would I turn into a fat couch potato?

.

3 – Sunday 24th April and looking ahead

Sunday 24th April had arrived. I eased myself out of bed and carefully slid down the stairs again. The pain wasn't so bad today, but I could still barely walk, let alone run a marathon. I returned to my temporary place of rest from yesterday, the sofa, I opened the sash window in the lounge; the sun was shining and a cool breeze flowed through the window and into the bright and airy room. I switched on the television at eight thirty and watched every minute of the London Marathon TV coverage until two in the afternoon. I felt like I was punishing myself by watching the thousands of runners work their way around the 26.2 mile course, but I just wanted to be part of the day that I had trained so hard for… The rest of Sunday passed by very slowly, hour by hour, as the dull pain continued to haunt me… How would I get to work on Monday? And what would I tell everybody in the office?

When Monday arrived, day three of the pain, it had reduced yet again. I'd been applying oil massage pads every six hours throughout the weekend, leaving the rooms in our house with a heady, perfumed aroma. I hobbled across the street and eased myself into my Audi .The weather was warm, the sky was blue and I had to put on a brave face to tell just about everybody in the office the same story of my misfortune over and over again. I drove the fifteen-mile journey to Bedford and pulled into the car park. Driving itself wasn't too painful, but getting in and out of the car was terrible. And now I had two flights of stairs to climb. Ouch… Aargghhhh…I was in excruciating pain by the time I arrived at my desk.

As I sat down I was greeted with the inevitable "How?", " Why?", "What happened?", "Oh dear", and "Oh my god!" comments. I responded to each and every one of my sympathetic work colleagues, trying to explain to each person who'd asked in as much detail as possible so they could understand my physical and emotional state. I felt really low and depressed after I'd settled down to work and was attending to my daily job of managing customers' computer systems. There were emails popping up on my screen from various friends, families and work colleagues who were yet to hear of my story .I sat asking myself the same question repeatedly: How would I move on from this injury? At this point I again began to feel lower still and didn't really want to think how long it would take for me to recover and get running again, let alone another marathon..

I made some enquiries at lunchtime about seeing my doctor and a managed to get an appointment for the next day at ten thirty. I wasn't hopeful of much more than a sports physio referral.

4 – The Lifeline

Later on in the afternoon, the owner of the company, Brian, walked into the office. He too had run a couple of marathons before. As I was hobbling down the office he invited me into his office for a 'marathon chat'. Brian and I would often discuss training tips, how far we had run each week and little findings during training that would help each other

I sat down and went through the whole story. I quickly saw that as a distance runner himself Brian knew how I was feeling. Quarter of an hour later, as I stood up to leave, he said "Stuart, there's always another marathon."

I agreed. Somehow I had to put things into perspective and clear my murky and misty outlook.

By about quarter to five that afternoon I felt drained, still in pain, and tired from another emotional day. My colleague Marilyn had just made me my final cup of tea of the day. I began typing an email and a bleep announced the arrival of a new email in my inbox. I glanced at the sender, and was surprised to see Brian's name. The subject title read "Interested?" Of course I was intrigued, so I opened the email and read the opening line: "Are you interested in running another marathon? If so, click on the link below..."

I couldn't think why Brian would send me an email link to the London Marathon 2012 when I'd explained a successful deferral. I felt excited but down, happy but sad as I clicked on the link.

Oh My Word! Shit!

I had to read the website that I had opened several times over. I smiled at my laptop... What a way to pick somebody up after hitting rock bottom! My colleagues glanced across at me and asked if I was ok. I just I replied that I'd read something funny as, frankly, I was in shock.

The site described an opportunity to run the 2011 New York City Marathon in November, six months from now. Brian and I would travel to New York and both run the NEW YORK marathon…Now that really did lift me; it lifted me so much that I read the email over and over…it contained guaranteed entry into the world's largest marathon on Sunday 6th November.

The idea was a three-night trip: fly to New York, stay in Times Square, run the marathon and then fly home on Monday 7th November. We'd be travelling with Sports International, a sports events company that guaranteed entry into the marathon.

I was in heaven. I even managed to spill my cup of tea across my desk through sheer excitement. For a ten-minute period, my injury was not there; I felt fine and the world looked so rosy. Just before I shut my laptop down for the day I read the email one more time and typed out a swift reply to Brian to confirm that I was interested. I typed YES in bold and made the suggestion that we discuss in more detail tomorrow.

The adrenaline rush that had provided brief respite wore off as I drove home; the pain returning. But I was on cloud nine right now…I couldn't wait to share this exciting piece of news to Lucy. I arrived home shortly after six, walked through the front door and into the kitchen where Lucy was preparing the dinner, a delicious-looking warm chicken salad. Lucy looked at me in amazement; she could see that something had changed since this morning.

But I contained my excitement and waited until we had dinner together before I explained the opportunity of a lifetime to run the New York marathon. Lucy was really pleased that I was smiling again, commenting that being down and negative didn't suit me. I sat on the sofa that night surfing the internet and avidly soaking up every detail I could find about the New

York City Marathon. That night I had the best night's sleep since my injury.

I woke up at seven am on Tuesday 26th April. I was going to see the doctor this morning for a diagnosis of my back injury. had to put New York to the back of my mind until I had received the prognosis of the injury and the rehabilitation I needed to be able to run again. I worked from home that morning before going to see Doctor Williams at eleven. It was actually the first time I had been to see this doctor since I'd moved to Hitchin six years previously. The doctor made a light-hearted joke about not actually meeting me before, I explained my injury, and then he asked me to perform a number of stretches to identify the source of the problem. After ten minutes of chatting and stretching, the doctor showed me which muscles had been damaged on the life-sized model skeleton standing against the wall. He recommended me to go and see a sports injury specialist. Phew...

He advised rough timescales of recovery but didn't want to commit until I had seen the therapist.

I returned home, called the sports therapist and made an appointment for Wednesday evening. Only a day to go to live with this pain until I would know what the future held. I got into my car, drove to the office and spent the rest of the day at my desk, my head buzzing with excitement that I might be going to New York for the biggest race of my life.

The next day came and went quickly, busy dealing with my day to day duties at the office. I returned home by six o'clock and spoke to Lucy about her day. Lucy worked as an interior designer in a bespoke kitchen shop called Planet Furniture, designing bespoke kitchens for wealthy clients. We chatted throughout dinner about what the sports physio was going to say in an hour or so.

I left the house just before eight in the evening and made the short journey around the corner to the sports physiotherapist called Think Physio, to see a highly recommended sports physiotherapist called Caroline Wilson. The session was booked at the local tennis club where Caroline practiced. It was a warm evening for this time of the year and I was dressed in my shorts, t-shirt and flip flops, knowing that I would be doing some gruelling stretches.

Just before quarter past eight Caroline opened the door of the treatment room and welcomed me in. I sat down and explained exact details of where my back problem started, and then went right through to my history of sports injuries over the years. Hopefully this would help to get to the source of the injury and not just treat the symptom. I had a good feeling about Caroline and the kind of information she was providing. I was asked to stretch this way and that way, bend forwards and backwards.

Caroline had diagnosed exactly where the problem was: a lower lumbar spine joint problem with muscle spasms in my lower left back, probably caused by the vigorous massage that I had received at the Marathon Expo on Friday.

The muscle spasm is called the facet joint and it was position L5/S1.. I was interested to hear the exact diagnosis of the injury - things like this always interested me - but I was even more interested in my rehab programme of exercises for a full recovery.

Caroline advised that my muscles, after being worked so hard over the last few months, had been extremely tight, even after stretching before and after each run. And then I go and have a massage that has in essence released the tension that had built up over those months. She also observed that the stiffness in my lower back when I leant forward might mean my core muscles were not as strong as they should be. That would surely have increased the risk of an injury like this, although it might have been caused by one of my numerous football injuries, knee, ankle, eye and shoulder operations. I felt relieved that the injury was quite common, but Caroline advised that back injuries can re-occur quite easily and it was vital I increase my core strength during my rehabilitation.

I was asked to lay on the treatment bed for some acupuncture. There were approximately 15 needles placed along my meridian lines to reduce the pain and discomfort of my lower back. As I lay there Caroline and I exchanged marathon stories; as her husband also runs the London Marathon each year we had plenty to discuss. The needles were removed after about 20 minutes of relaxing, followed by some massage to put the muscle back to where it should be; the sickening, dull pain was being caused by a trapped muscle. Caroline applied pressure very slowly over the affected area; even with my high pain threshold I could still feel the pain.

Finally, my lower back was taped with some large sticky bandage tape to keep my back tight after the acupuncture and the massage. The massage had left me quite sore where the muscles had been manipulated, but the overall result was very encouraging as I felt I had turned the corner in my road to recovery.

I sat up with my back feeling tight from the tape. It was the first time in five days that I felt normal again. Caroline recommended that I buy a fit ball and use it to perform some core exercises to strengthen my inner core muscles and by association build more strength in my lower back. I had to be careful in the future. I left the treatment room with a spring in my step again - not literally, at this stage, as I had to take it easy. I had a follow-up appointment in a week, if I felt I needed it.

I had been given strict instructions that I could start running again in a few days, providing I do my core training with the fit ball twice a day. This would then allow me to go for some gentle ten to fifteen-minute runs a really slow pace.. I was impatient to begin, but fully aware that I shouldn't overdo it.

It was business as usual with work on Thursday again, another busy day getting through with lots of problem-solving and keeping the customers happy. This had been quite a challenge when training for a marathon; with the amount of effort you have to put in when working five days a week and training five nights per week, it was a big ask to cram it all in. I'd been unaware that it had taken over my life to a point, but the realisation is the key to succeeding in these types of challenges.

The following day was a public holiday in the UK, with the Royal Wedding taking place on Friday 29th April. So Friday morning would be a perfect opportunity to go for a run in a relaxed frame of mind rather than the usual scramble to squeeze it in after a full day at work
It was slightly overcast at nine in the morning on the day of the Royal Wedding between Kate and William, which was scheduled for midday. I pulled on my running gear for the first time in over a week, slightly nervous about how my first run would go. I didn't want to overdo it and injure myself, or it might be the end for me..I set off at a very slow pace, taking the first steps from my house extremely carefully.

There was no pain. Should there be?

I continued down the road for five minutes, increasing the pace slightly so I was running at about ten per cent of my normal pace.

It felt good...

I continued on for about another five to seven minutes, not wanting to do too much, and then returned home. My first run had been successful. I then used the fit ball to perform my core strengthening again; this was essential before and after each exercise. I felt so positive after this session and vowed to repeat this again in a couple of days.

I showered and then Lucy and I went to visit our friends Russell and Freya to watch the Royal Wedding on TV and have a few glasses of champagne. It was a delightful and relaxing day. Mid-afternoon, Lucy and I went round to visit her parents, Den & Lyn. Den was in the middle of renovating their main bathroom and was putting some old reworked wooden beams on the walls. I had offered to help a couple weeks prior to the marathon, but of course Den was now working on his own. He asked if I could help with holding one of the beams in place; I did so, being careful and aware of my injury. I held the wooden beam up for about 30 seconds but then felt a slight twinge in my back and immediately put it down. Had I been really stupid, pushed my luck and gone back a step? I became worried that I had undone the good work I'd begun.

Later on that evening I emailed Caroline to see if I could make an emergency appointment on Saturday morning after my scare. I was in luck, Caroline emailed me and confirmed ten-thirty appointment.

The next day, Saturday 30th April, the temperature was again unusually high for this time of the year and I was going to see Chelsea play West Ham in a crucial Premiership League game in the afternoon. I had plenty of time to get to London for the three o'clock kickoff.

I waited patiently to be greeted by Caroline again. This time, as she opened the door to her treatment room, her face was set in a more serious expression. She, like I, might have been remembering her specific advice not to do any lifting, given only a couple of days ago.
I sat down in the warm treatment room, and explained what I'd done. Why *did* I do that? Nonetheless, Caroline was still very pleased with the progress I had made and my treatment this time was more a deep massage in the affected area of my lower back. Again I felt a dull yet sickening pain, but my back felt a lot easier. Caroline also observed that the affected areas didn't seem to be so tight compared to three days ago. Phew; I thought I had gone backwards, but fortunately I'd scraped

through, no doubt helped by the core exercises I'd been performing.

I thanked Carline for her work and for fitting me in at short notice. She advised further exercise; more of the gentle runs with a view to extending them bit by bit but without overdoing it.

I walked to the railway station and took the train to London with a huge sigh of relief. I also started to believe that I could begin my New York training soon, as I still had six months to go; plenty of time to focus and train correctly to ensure that I would avoid an injury.

I met with my good mate Terry at a pub at Fulham Broadway, just a few minutes' walk from the stadium. We had a couple of cool beers on this hot, sunny day and discussed the game ahead and who would win...Chelsea needed to beat West Ham and then keep winning to stand an outside chance of retaining the Premier League. They went on to win three-nil. I returned home in good spirits and spent the evening having dinner with Lucy and relaxing.

5 – Training through the summer

Back at work in early May, Brian and I finalised the trip to New York. Now the hard work of getting fit would begin.

I had a little over six months to take another bite of the cherry. I continued to walk around on cloud nine for the next few days, having received confirmation from Sports International that we were actually going. I often sat at my desk wondering what it would be like running through the famous five boroughs of New York. I wanted to make this happen for the obvious personal reasons, but it also meant a lot to me that both Brian and I were going to take on this amazing challenge.

I browsed the internet for marathon training plans, diets, alcohol intake advice, watches, running clothing and more; it took me nearly four weeks to complete my research. I had worked out that I would start my training plan in July as I had a couple of weekend breaks away in Cheltenham and Exeter. So in reality I couldn't concentrate fully on my training plan to run the marathon in under four hours. That was my ultimate goal and I could feel my emotions unsettle when I considered the way the possibilities had shifted: from under four hours to over four hours; just to finish, just to take part; and then to three and a half hours... No way, surely I couldn't finish in three and a half hours could I? I shook my head. Just concentrate on the realistically achievable.

From early June until early August the temperatures in my corner of Hertfordshire soared up to 35 degrees at times. Even in the evenings, as I started running several six-mile runs each week, it was often 25 degrees and the humidity high. So I was always sweating buckets and really feeling the heat; not my best running conditions at all.

As the weeks passed I increased my distance to eight miles with a few five-mile runs per week too. I was averaging 23 miles per week, a good solid start, according to distance running specialist Hal Higdon's training plan.

My pace at this distance was a slow eight minutes and twenty seconds per mile over an eight-mile distance, which I was happy with initially. I found it difficult in these sweltering conditions to improve my pace, so I would have to wait until the temperature cooled in September and October. My calculations were telling me that I was not going to manage a four-hour marathon at this current pace and with this mentality.

Something had to change. I needed to start increasing my pace; otherwise it would take a miracle to break the four hour barrier. And I really wanted to be in the sub four-hour club of runners.

Over the next few days, mostly during my lunch breaks at work, I spent several hours researching the internet. I found and bought a book called *4 months to a 4 hour marathon*, written by David Kuehls. Unfortunately I found it a little basic for my needs; it didn't tell me anything I hadn't already learnt.

The one thing I *did* identify was that each of the marathon-running books I looked at had been written by somebody who wasn't working five days per week in a nine-to-five job like me. These books simply were not a true representation of how to train successfully for a marathon. They didn't present a realistic view of what you had to do to complete a marathon in under four hours while working in a regular job.

And that's the main reason I set out to write this book. I want to share my experiences with everyone to prove that *anybody* can do it if they put their mind to it.

So this book will always explain how I managed to accommodate my training with a five-day working week. What's more, I was on-call for the customer's systems at Bluechip, the IT engineering company where I worked. That meant that for one whole week in every five I could be contacted by a customer at any time of day or night. That could mean interrupted sleep at just the time I needed it least.

So how did I fit my increased training plan into my busy work life?

Typically I would wake up at ten to seven Monday to Friday, have a bowl of cereal and drink plenty of water before travelling the 25-minute car journey to Bluechip in Bedford.

I would usually grab a sandwich and fruit for lunch and munch on a couple of biscuits with several cups of tea each day. To fuel my evening runs I would also have a banana at about half-four, leaving enough time for me to digest it.

I would usually go for my evening run as soon as I got home from work – usually about quarter past six, and then eat dinner at about quarter to eight. I ran shorter runs nightly from Monday to Thursday, rested on Friday and go for my long run on a Saturday or Sunday.

It was now mid-August, so I had two and a half months to start improving my pace and extending my distances so that eventually I could sustain a fast enough pace over the distance of 26.2 miles. I needed to follow a strict training plan. Two and a half months isn't long and each week seemed to be flying by before I knew it.

I finally made my decision on the choice of the marathon training plan. It was devised by Hal Higdon, a famous American runner who has run many marathons. The plan was based over seven days and aimed at the intermediate runner. I put myself into this category as I really wanted to raise the bar and push myself. The plan suited my lifestyle and the days that I was already running. I thought if I followed the schedule as much as possible, I wouldn't go far wrong.

As each week went by, I was racking up the miles, completing from 20 to 45 miles each week. I had to purchase another pair of my favourite trainers, ASICS Gel Kayano 17, as I started to increase my mileage. Most experts say you should be able to get three to four hundred miles out of a pair of trainers before you should change them or run a greater risk of injury. Normally I can get four hundred miles out of a pair of the Gel Kayano trainers before I feel the tarmac of the road, but running 40 miles a week meant I was wearing them out more quickly than usual. As ever when running a marathon distance, I bought my trainers one size up from my usual size.

I liked the Hal Higdon training plan; it was pushing me to increase the miles and I was really enjoying the challenge. I was up to fifteen miles as my weekly long run by the beginning of September. I updated my training progress spreadsheet on a daily basis and checked to see my next distance and the pace that I should be running it at: marathon pace, fartlek, or an easy run.

There were some instances where I decided not to run on a Saturday to give my body an extra day's rest before the long run, heading out instead on a Sunday. If I felt like a rest then I would have a rest. I decided to listen to what my body was telling me. I was beginning to ache every night when I was running four nights in a row and I felt shattered once I had sat down on the sofa after dinner.

Socially, at this stage of my marathon training I was still drinking a fair amount of alcohol, mostly beer and wine on a Friday and Saturday. But my long runs were not improving as much as I would have liked. I recognised that this had to be affected by my alcohol intake the night before. The longer I continued to drink alcohol, the less likely it was that I'd improve my overall pace enough to break the four-hour barrier.

6 – Fitness Review

It was time to review my fitness and my progress, and something had to change for me to further improve my performance. My pace per mile had improved, according to the MapMyRUN phone app that I used to measure my training runs, distance, pace, calories burnt and so on. I had improved from 8.30 minutes per mile to 8.10, but I still had a long way to go to ensure I finished in less than four hours. To guarantee a finish in under four hours I had to run at an average of nine minutes per mile over the entire 26.2 miles. This would give me a finish of 3 hours and 56 minutes, but that didn't give me much room for tiredness, and besides, I wanted to be better than that. I wanted to be much quicker so there was some slack in the time. My improvement in three weeks had been pretty good, which I put down to following Hal's training plan.

I decided to cut down on my alcohol intake on a Friday night if I was doing my long run early on Saturday morning. I was trying to run at a similar time that I'd aim for in New York. The weather in September was still unusually warm for this time of the year, so I had to ensure I was still drinking lots of water to keep myself hydrated throughout my long runs. As I increased my long runs to eighteen miles, I noticed that historically my pace dipped rapidly after I had reached the fifteen-mile marker, and my thighs tightened with what felt like cramp in my thighs. A work colleague, Steve, who is a very keen time trial cyclist recommended I take some Zero Sport hydration tablets before and during a race to ensure my body would be fully hydrated. I chose the lime-flavoured ones. I tried them on my next long run, dropping each into a pint of water and taking one thirty minutes before the run and the next at fourteen miles if I felt any tightness or 'hit the wall'.

With seven weeks to go, my pace had improved to around eight minutes per mile up to a distance of fifteen miles and I had also conquered hitting the wall by introducing the hydration tablets. I really felt I had achieved some quick wins that would allow me to further improve my performance over the coming weeks.

Again, rather pleased with my progress since mid-August when I'd started following Hal Higdon's training plan, I found myself logged onto the Runners World website forum and picking up a few tips. Many runners' comments were advising real race practice by running a few 10K races or half-marathons, to feel the pressure of a real race again, to assess my progress and measure my improvement against fellow runners. I searched the internet for some available and local half-marathons. I found the Oxford Half-Marathon, which was due to place on Saturday 24th September 2011 with a nine-thirty start time. It was only just over an hour's drive from where we live. I applied online and paid my £24 fee. The Oxford Half is a fairly flat course so I would be able to measure my progress and review my areas of development. It was also an interesting course, beginning at the Oxford United football stadium, and on through the centre of Oxford past its beautiful, historic buildings before returning back to the stadium.

7 - Race Practice Oxford Half

It was Wednesday 20th September when I received my running number and timing chip through the post for the Oxford Half. Strangely enough, I felt nervous about the race, perhaps as I hadn't run many races and I was used to running on my own when I trained. I knew the moment that I signed up that I was taking this running training very seriously, as it was taking up a fair amount of my free time now. But I needed to invest time and effort into this if I was going to succeed on Sunday 6th November in New York.

After all I wanted to be as fit as I possibly could, so I could run and enjoy the New York marathon rather than hit the wall by seventeen miles and be totally exhausted, as I had been in previous marathons. This race would confirm how good I was, how I compared to fellow runners, confirm my current pace, and show me how to improve on my pace over a distance of thirteen miles to be ready for New York, identify my areas of development and learn from my mistakes.

Lucy and I decided to make a weekend of it by travelling to Oxford on the Saturday and staying at a nearby hotel on the city outskirts. Before we left I packed my running gear along with the Lucozade, Carbo Gels that I generally consume every hour when doing my longer runs, and my hydration tablets. It took just over an hour to get there, and the weather was overcast with the temperature hovering at around nineteen degrees, comfortable running weather I thought.

At this stage of my training I was eating salads and fruit at lunchtime every weekday, so I was beginning to lose weight; something that I needed to do to ensure I was as light on my feet as possible. I normally weighed in at 13st 9lbs before I started increasing my training, but the pounds were dropping off from healthier eating and less alcohol.

My simple philosophy was this: if I was one stone heavier than I wanted to be in a marathon, I would be carrying twenty-six stone extra over one mile or an extra stone over twenty-six miles... Whichever you look at it, it makes a real difference to be as trim as possible.

My mindset was good as we arrived in the city centre of Oxford after checking in at the hotel. It was lunchtime, the sun was out yet again, and the temperature was around 22 degrees,

When would this warm weather ever end? Lucy and I chose a restaurant where I had a chicken salad without dressing, I really wanted to be as fit as possible now in these last few weeks as I had seen improvements in my pace and increased distances due to losing weight. We wandered around the shops in the city centre, but I kept running the next day's race through my mind. My nerves had just started to kick in.

Lucy's parents Den and Lyn had also made the trip to support me and cheer me on at the end of the race. That evening the four of us met for dinner at a seafood restaurant called Loch Fyne in Church Street, nestled in a cosmopolitan area of Oxford with several trendy bars and restaurants. We went for a drink in a nearby wine bar before dinner. At this point I thought I would have a couple of glasses of wine; surely that wouldn't affect me; it was a moderate amount compared to my previous intake.

So I knew my boundaries, and as I was running quicker I knew that I would be ok. The restaurant was a very noisy place and all of us opted for the restaurant's speciality seafood dishes. I chose sea bass with steamed vegetables, a light and healthy option, along with regular glasses of water throughout the evening to ensure I was fully hydrated. We returned to the hotel by half ten as I wanted a good night's sleep to ensure I was ready for the 13.1 mile run. The weather was going to be sunny and warm AGAIN, up to twenty-four degrees, so it was pretty warm for autumn.

On Sunday 24th September, my alarm went off at seven. I had to leave at eight to drive the short distance to the Kassam Football Stadium. I showered and went to breakfast, where I drank a sweet cup of tea and ate two slices of toast with strawberry preserve. It was a little tip I had seen on the internet; good carbs and plenty of energy. I returned to my hotel room, changed into my running gear and said goodbye to Lucy, who was going to travel with her parents to the finish line to cheer me on. I really felt nervous, but why?

It was only a half-marathon, with two and a half thousand people running, so what was I nervous about? I couldn't put my finger on it really, but I was slightly concerned about drinking enough fluids, either too much or too little before the race. Was I concerned about being hydrated enough, maybe? Or more worried about the number of times I would have to go for a pee before the race?

I arrived at half past eight with plenty of time to spare, following the bright yellow Oxford Half-Marathon parking signs and parking up next to a long line of cars. I gathered my belongings, locked up and followed the crowds to the registration and warm-up area and familiarised myself with the amenities, and the bag drop area.

At this relatively early hour the sun was out but the temperature was a cool eleven degrees. I picked my spot in the registration area to keep warm and performed my intense stretching routine, along with drinking my hydration sports drink as recommended by my work colleague, Steve the keen cyclist. I relaxed while I stretched. My head felt right, even though I had drunk three glasses of wine (why bother drinking at all!) the night before?

As nine o'clock approached, I cast my eye surreptitiously at the other runners; many looked nervous and quite a few looked very fit.

Shortly after nine I went for my first toilet stop, the first of six visits before the race There was a shortage of toilets in the registration area so I wandered outside in search of more; surely at a football stadium like this...? The race officials were pointing the runners to use the stadium toilets...Phew, panic over!

At nine thirty I wandered away from the stadium and made my way to the start line, about a two-minute stroll around the corner. The beat of the music could be heard several hundred feet away: a DJ with some SL10 decks and two large subwoofer speakers blasting out some jazz funk tunes to get the runners in the right frame of mind.

I was there already.

I arrived at the start, where I discovered that there were no starting markers for predicted finish times. I found this very unusual; it meant this would be a free-for-all. Lots of the slower runners were near the front so the faster runners might not be able to get off to such a good start. I stood near the front and caught sight of the famous British marathon runner Liz Yelling, who was waiting patiently at the front. I overheard lots of fellow runners describing hoped-for PB times (meaning personal best) of sub-75 minutes...I glanced around and all I could see was a lot of elite runners, so I shuffled backwards discreetly to feel more comfortable among the slightly less accomplished runners.

After a fifteen-minute delay due to traffic congestion, the Oxford Half-Marathon was ready to start

BANG!

The gun blasted and the race had begun. As I crossed the start line I pressed 'start' on my iPhone MapMyRUN app, before pushing the phone into my waist-belt zip bag and into the top of my shorts. It was a bit uncomfortable at times but at least I could measure my pace. In the space of an hour the temperature had risen to nineteen degrees and I could feel the sun strong all over the back of my neck and exposed shoulders and arms.

The first mile was flat, past a residential area. I felt like I was going too fast, and a quick check of my phone revealed that I was: a pace of six minutes fifty. As usual I'd got carried away among the other runners. Map My Run flashed up the alerted 'Slow Down". I dropped my pace to 8.20 minutes per mile, the training pace which had felt comfortable.

It seemed that there were loads of runners overtaking me I allowed them to pass without 'biting' again. I turned left past the Rover/Mini car factory and hit the three-mile point, feeling better for the slower pace. I took on my first water. The 330ml bottles were huge, too big to run with, but in this heat I needed it all. I poured some over the back of my neck and the rest I drank.

The next three miles were really tough and boring: flat dual carriageway with nothing to see. I plodded on and on and began to struggle as the temperature hit 24 degrees. I felt a bit of tightness in my chest due to the heat and, I suspect, the alcohol from the previous night. I slowed down further to an 8.30 pace so I could ease through the next couple of miles, and miles four and five passed without too much trouble.

At the half way point I took on another giant water bottle, again pouring some over my head as I was sweating heavily. With just a light breeze in the air I was still very hot, but just about managing to cope and maintain my 8.30 pace.

I ran down a long hill that was shaded, allowing me to increase my pace and get in the zone again. I returned to an eight minute mile speed, something that had felt right during my recent raining sessions and which I felt I could maintain this during the next few miles.

Miles seven, eight and nine came quickly. Nobody seemed to be passing me now and I'd settled into a good rhythm as I weaved my way through the cobbled streets of historic Oxford.

There were over 2,500 runners in this race and I was wondering how many of them were in front of me as I took in the sights of Oxford. It's just one of the many strange thoughts that you have during a race. I continued through to the south side of the city alongside the canal and then along another dual carriageway.

I reached mile ten, my pace was good and I was taking on plenty of water at each water stop to ensure I kept hydrated and as cool as possible in these tough conditions. I felt stronger than ever at this point and quite a few runners that had passed me during mile two and mile three were either walking or struggling with new injuries, calf and hamstring strains. Some looked in absolute agony. I felt a slight hunger pain, so took my first Lucozade Carbo Gel to get some fuel onboard for the last three miles. I knew this was a vital point in the race for me. At just over ten and a half miles, I knew from my training that I could maintain an eight-minute mile pace over the two and a half miles to the finish, so the Carbo Gel had helped at the right time.

Another cycle path, followed by three roundabouts before going under an underpass. I was passing tens of runners at this stage and I felt great inside. I even smiled to myself that I had run a sensible race in this heat and reduced my speed at the right time to allow me to finish strong.

I hit the twelve-mile mark and took on my final water, before showering my hot head with the remainder of the cold water; it felt so nice, so refreshing!. I was sure I was going to finish with a good time after my slow pace between miles two and three.

I reached into my waist belt to check my time on my iPhone as I was nearing the finish. It was becoming a little awkward, an extra weight and discomfort, and now the phone was wet with sweat and water.

I turned the final corner and felt like I was sprinting now, probably reaching a pace of 7.15 minutes a mile.

I could hear the commentator over the loudspeaker in the football stadium shouting their names as each runner was crossing the finish line.

I knew that Lucy, Den and Lyn would be waiting at the finish line inside the stadium. I turned into the stadium and caught sight of them as I sprinted down the finishing straight, passing the line with a rush of relief and adrenaline, with a big grin on my face.

Phew! I had finished in one hour and forty-three minutes> I'd averaged 7.56 minutes per mile and, especially considering the heat, I was really pleased with my overall performance.

I actually managed to forget to perform my post-race stretches as I chatted to Lucy and her folks, telling them all about the each stage of the race. I wiped and dried the sweat from my iPhone. I really *had* to find a better solution before New York to monitor my pace and time.

I went to the nearby LA Fitness gym to take a shower and throw on fresh clothes. Lucy and I left Oxford and stopped off at Bicester's shopping retail park for some lunch.

I didn't feel any aches or strains from the race, just very warm. A good days' work…
The next few weeks were going to be very important if I was to break the four-hour barriers in New York. Today was one hour forty-three, so that's a pace of three hours and twenty-six minutes, as a rough guide. Something to aim for anyway.

What could I do to improve before the big day in November?

8 – The next few weeks' training

One thing I had noticed was that I felt lighter when I was running, in training and in my recent half-marathon in Oxford. But I needed to feel even lighter on my feet. I decided that I would buy a GPS sports watch rather than having a waist belt and iPhone weighing me down. Why hadn't I done this before? All of these small changes would help me surely? Perhaps it was just the experience of taking part in a race - I'd seen what other runners were wearing and doing, picking up so many good ideas and tips.

I spent the next few lunch breaks at work each day researching the best GPS running watch to buy. The information these watches would deliver was incredible: time, distance, calories, current pace, average pace, best pace, last pace... this would be another small change to put me in a good position for the Big Apple.

I chose the Garmin 305, setting me back just £89 online at Amazon, which seemed to have a big selection of running gear at great prices.

I never looked back after buying the watch. It had everything I needed and more. I could even download my runs to my computer and analyse each and every mile to see where I'd peaked and where I'd dipped.

The watch turned me into a bit of a statistician. It became an obsession. As an example, I would always check my average pace as soon as I'd completed a run when using the MapMyRUN app, but the Garmin 305 made me examine every little detail. I used to think "What's twenty seconds here or there?" But the new watch made me realise that every second is so crucial.

With my latest purchase I could push myself to go even quicker to ensure I break the four-hour barrier.

9 – Letchworth 10K - 2nd October

My next step was another race before New York, as I'd felt a huge benefit from the Oxford race. I decided on the annual 10K Standalone Farm run held just up the road from me in Letchworth, Hertfordshire, where about 1,500 runners would be competing.

A good friend of mine, Craig, and his partner Therese were visiting from Sweden, so a group of us met up on the Saturday night. I was conscious that I would be running the next morning, but as I was also aware that I'd reached a high level of fitness I was happy enough to drink two pints of Peroni that evening at a new bar called The Hermitage, a gastro type bar and restaurant that had recently opened in Hitchin. We followed that up with a really tasty Thai meal nearby. Lucy and I left the Thai restaurant around at about eleven pm and went home and off to bed. I managed to get a good night's sleep considering the temperature had reached twenty-seven degrees that day.

If you're wondering why I'm describing the minutiae of my life in this way, don't worry, it's all relevant. I was shortly to take on a huge personal fitness challenge, and I want to provide a truthful and open account of every factor that would play a part. I held down a busy, sometimes stressful job, had a reasonably active social life, and was training hard too. But just because I was in preparation mode, I didn't feel I had to sacrifice everything – including little pleasures such as good food and moderate intake of alcohol.

The next day was Sunday 2nd October and again the heat was high. I remember thinking about how warm it had been throughout the last six months of training, and that was something that I simply wasn't used to; all my training for previous races had taken place between November and April.

Lucy and I woke at half seven and had a light breakfast of cornflakes and a cup of tea. We drove the ten-minute journey to Letchworth and parked in a nearby field given over to parking.

Lucy was also running today. She's a keen runner, but she doesn't allow it to take over her life and only takes part in nearby 10Ks. Perhaps that's because she's a creative person, an interior designer and, in my experience at least, a creative person is very rarely a sportsperson.

We waited on the hill at the start of the race. We could feel the heat building even at twenty past nine. I had taken my hydration sports drink even though it was only a short distance.

I lined up at the 45-minute marker as I was looking to run the 10K in around this time. I was aware though that the heat might yet be a factor in my finishing time. I gave Lucy a kiss, and we wished each other luck before she made her way her way to the one-hour marker.

I bumped into a few friends, all around eight years younger than me and relatively new to running, but keen to improve. We exchanged a few jokes about the race, who would beat who and so on, before readying ourselves for the start.

The gun went off at precisely nine forty-five. The race had begun. I pressed the start on my Garmin 305 watch and set off.

The course went down into a dip before a fairly steep uphill climb for about 400 yards. My chest felt tight again... was it the heat or was it the alcohol from the previous night? I should really learn not to drink the night before. As I reached the top of the hill, my watch bleeped to inform me I was going too fast: a pace of 6.50 after mile one. I eased off the pace for the second mile, where the course was flat and slightly downhill, still wishing for a breeze or some shade.

I was in a good zone for mile three, though the water stop couldn't come quick enough, and I was dripping with sweat and gasping for a cool breeze. The friends I'd been chatting with at the start were just in front of me, although one had sprinted ahead into the distance.

I turned left after the water stop and onto a dual carriageway. The sun beat down directly onto me, as the temperature reached 27 degrees. All I wanted now was another water stop to see me though to the end of the race. As I turned a corner I was relieved to see the water stop so near I managed to get two cups of water: one for my thirst and one for my head.

At mile five it was time to see how much progress I had made in the last six months. I increased my speed to an average pace of 7.20 minutes per mile for the last mile and passed tens of runners who'd set off too fast again.

I felt good again at this point. In fact, it was starting to feel normal that I felt so good at the end of a race. I rounded the last corner, entered the farm, and passed the finish line.

45 minutes and 21 seconds. Not bad for such a hot day, so I was fairly pleased...

I waited at the finish line for Lucy to come through. Her time two years ago was 66 minutes, but with her recent training I was hoping she could get close to the hour mark. It wasn't too long before I caught sight of her as approaching the finish. She was smiling and wasn't even sweating, and I shouted her name as she came through in 61 minutes. It was a huge improvement for Lucy, who is only a social runner and when you consider the 27 degrees of heat, a great achievement.

We returned home, showered and changed as we had close family for lunch and a BBQ to take advantage of the late hot weather.

It was the 2nd October, and I resolved that today would be my last day of drinking beer until New York if I wanted to be as fit and as light as possible.

So, five weeks to lose weight, stay sharp and improve my average pace.

I calculated that a pint of beer is 300 calories, so to cut out the booze entirely for five weeks would be a great saving.

The family BBQ went well and I drank too many beers in the hot sun, but it would be the last time for a while…

10 – Last Few Weeks of Training

The training plan was nearing its finale. In fact this coming Sunday, the 9th October, would be my longest training run of 20 miles before I began my tapering off process.

I was still very strict with my daily diet: a bowl of crunchy nut cornflakes, no snacking on biscuits with my cups of tea, a healthy chicken salad containing around 250 calories with a bowl of fruit, followed by a banana at half-four in the afternoon.

This would see me through until I returned home from work ready for my evening run at six fifteen. Generally sticking to Hal Higdon's training plan Monday's run was 4.6 miles; a nice country lane run which I completed in about 34 minutes, with a 7.35 minute per mile pace.

"WOW..." I thought. "How has my pace improved so much?"

I just didn't understand what had happened for me to be running much quicker than only a few weeks previously. Perhaps my pace was good over a short distance but would then dip after so many miles…

I took Tuesday off as a rest day, as frankly I felt shattered from a hectic day at work. I'd allowed myself on occasion to swap my rest days around to fit in with my lifestyle, although I'd never have two days off in a row.

I did the same 4.6-mile country run on Wednesday with an average pace of 7.38 minutes a mile. Pretty close to my previous run, so I had definitely improved somehow. Was it down to my watch, the two races that I had completed, or my diet and weight loss?

That Saturday, the 8th October, I decided to change my twenty mile long run to a fast thirteen mile run to see if I could maintain my recent fast pace compared to two weeks ago at Oxford.

I ran the thirteen mile distance in an improved time of one hour forty-two minutes. Two minutes quicker than before; I was happy with that. Although I hadn't completed the recommended 20 miles today, I knew I was improving in other areas very quickly.

Part of me wished that I had discovered these new tips earlier in my training, then I would be running even faster by now. Surely there'd be a limit to my improvement though; there must be some point where my body could not go any quicker while I maintained my normal lifestyle.

I worked from home on Monday 10th October as I had to complete some project work without being disturbed. In the evening I decided to go for my favourite 8.63 run (a third of a full marathon). This run was a mixture of hill, flat and downhill.

My time was one hour six minutes, my pace was 7.41 minutes a mile. So I knew I was maintaining the pace as I increased my distance, but what I wanted to know was the distance at which my pace would drop off. That was the area I'd need to concentrate on.

My only concern at this stage was that I hadn't completed enough long runs. But I was really pleased with all the other areas of my training so I wasn't going to let it get to me; I knew that I was very strong and feeling as fit as when I used to play football in my early twenties.

On Tuesday I did my regular 4.6-mile country run at the slightly slower pace of 7.53. Perhaps I was feeling the effects of the last few days' hard and fast runs.
On Wednesday I went for a slow pace of 10.30. I was running country lane run with Lucy; once in a while I found it really good to go for a slow run, to stretch the muscles while running a slower pace.

11 – Final Long Run: 18 Miles

On Saturday 16th October I was scheduled to complete my last long run of eighteen miles, the continuation of my taper in my training program.

Today was the big test for me. No alcohol the previous night; in fact a bowl of pasta, followed by a good eight hours' sleep and some toast and jam as my breakfast, followed by the sports hydration drink I always take about thirty minutes before my run. This would be the biggest test of how far I had progressed with distance, pace and time.

I left the house at twenty past eight, pressed the start button on my watch and set off. It was sunny but fresh, which I hoped would be the kind of weather I'd have in New York.

I started well, and as I went my watch bleeped and pointed out that I was either 'too fast' or 'too slow'. This would be a test of how far I could run before my pace dipped and when I might hit the wall in the marathon...

Well WOW...

I was shocked and over the moon. I ran a distance of 17.83 miles in a time of two hours twenty; a pace of 7.57 minutes a mile.

I felt on top of the world. This was my best run ever... I had just calculated that if I had continued at the same pace my full marathon time would be 3 hours thirty-eight. Now I would be elated with that result in three weeks' time.

My mind was running away with itself, but I came back down to earth with a bump when the aches and pains started to set in...

Later that evening Lucy and I had dinner and I had a few glasses of an Australian Sauvignon Blanc, but passed on the beer. I slept well but kept thinking about New York as it was only three weeks away. I rested on Sunday in recognition of my improvement. I still couldn't put my finger on exactly what was different about my fitness, but I was definitely faster.

My only conclusion was that the consistent pace of each run was allowing my body to be tuned; I would switch off when I got home from work and 'click' into gear during my training runs.

12 – My Final Discovery: Hill Training

It was Monday 17th October and I continued to use Hal Higdon's training plan as much as possible, unless my body was telling me otherwise.

While I was on my lunch break I was again researching marathon tips on the internet and came across the elevation of the New York course.

WOW...

I logged onto the official ING New York City Marathon website and was shocked by the number of hills and bridges that awaited me. Generally I don't do hills very well...

I realised I'd really need to push myself if I wanted to break the four-hour barrier, especially now that I knew there'd be several steep climbs.

I was so determined to achieve this. I was totally focused. I continued on my strict diet of cereal, fruit and a healthy salad, followed by more fruit. Perhaps this was my secret.

I studied the course map and thought hard.

I had cracked it... Later that day I would strengthen my quads by introducing some hill training to my plan, something I'd not seriously considered before.

Several people had previously suggested I should do the hill running, but I never thought that this would improve my fitness...How wrong could somebody ever be?!

It was a cooler evening of around 12 degrees. I ran into the town centre and found a hill called Hollow Lane, which incorporated a 400-metre steep incline, followed by a 400-metre downhill run with a flat stretch. I decided to complete a further four laps. This would really sort the men from the boys.

It helped my heart rate when I reached the top of the hills, but most importantly this would strengthen my quads... What an amazing feeling.

After completing four hills circuits I returned home with another hill sprint, albeit one with a lesser incline. I was shattered when I pressed the stop button on my watch; quite clearly the difference between this and my usual runs was greater than I'd imagined, and was engaging my core muscles more too.

I felt pumped. Was this the secret to taking on the big bridges of New York?

Surely this would be my last discovery before the big race. Looking back, I realised just how much more I'd found out over the last four weeks alone. Part of me was asking "Why did I not discover these new tips much earlier on in my training?"

I guess I hadn't ploughed so much hard work and effort into investigating distance running advantages in the dispirited aftermath of my injury before the London Marathon. The determination I now felt was very different to the way I'd approached my previous marathons.

I felt good inside, and went to bed with a smile on my face, thinking I had found something that would surely allow me to break the four-hour barrier. Soon though, my thoughts turned negative and I pondered on the possibility of having a bad run or, worse still, picking up a late injury. With just three weeks to go, London was playing on my mind.

Back at work again on Tuesday 17th October, I chatted with Brian. We were exchanging training tips on a regular basis. This was Brian's first New York marathon too, so we shared the same excitement, and both of us were slightly nervous about what to expect, given the possible jetlag that might accompany us before and during the race.

It was another hectic day in the office and I didn't get away until later than planned. A hard day at work would often upset my mindset, so I decided not to run that night. I believe it's pointless running if you don't feel right... My body would give out signals to remind me when I felt tired.

I'd been following Hal Higdon's training plan down to the finest detail initially, but as time went on if I didn't feel like training , then I would simply skip a day. I didn't try to do twice the distance the following day as that would increase the risk of injury.

I resumed my training on Wednesday night after work, doing my favourite 1/3 of a marathon distance of 8.63 miles. Over the past month or so my times had been improving with all of the tips I had picked up and tonight I clocked a time of one hour five minutes at a pace of 7.35 minutes per mile. This was a superb performance; the hill training must be paying off already and my mind was still fully focused.

I rested on Thursday and Friday; even had some wine with dinner on the Thursday night. How much longer could I hold out before returning to my 'normal' lifestyle of wine, beer and the occasional takeaway? All in moderation though; it had only been one month really since I'd changed my food and alcohol intake.

It was only three weeks until I could have a large cold beer, wine and a Chinese takeaway. Lucy continued to support me by only having the occasional glass of wine, and it was her support and jokes on that topic kept me going when I really wanted to have a beer.

13 – My Final Two Weeks

I decided that in the last two weeks I concentrate on quality running and not quantity from now on. I was tapering off and my next long run was due on Saturday.

It was my long distances that were concerning me slightly. In this training plan I had only run twenty miles once and several eighteen-mile runs, whereas I'd finished plenty of thirteen-mile runs at pace. Was it going to be enough to see me through on the big day?

On Saturday 22nd October I was scheduled to run another thirteen-miler. I liked my thirteen-miler as I could combine my favourite 8.63 (third of a marathon) with my 4.85-mile country lane run to make up the 13.1 miles. I liked both routes as they provided a bit of variety to test me.

I set off at just after eight am, the weather much cooler now at about eight degrees, similar to the likely New York weather. I wore the running gear that I would be wearing on Sunday 6th November to ensure it felt right; no rubbing, chaffing etc

It was another great run for me personally and turned out to be a PB: an hour and forty-one minutes. I had improved by just under four minutes since the Oxford half I returned home and performed my stretches in the back garden. Then I sat on the cream wooden bench and smiled up to the sky, closed my eyes and sat still for five minutes to relax. This set me up for the rest of the day.

That evening Lucy and I invited some friends over for dinner, followed by wine again and a couple of cheeky vodkas, but I steered clear of the beer. There was a pattern forming now, alcohol in moderation seemed to be working, whereas it would have been extremely difficult to train with excessive alcohol intake.

I would normally rest on Sundays, but I felt I needed to put some more miles in the bank as I hadn't performed enough long runs. It was about three o'clock in the afternoon when I get to get changed, but suddenly a big wave of tiredness kicked in. Should I go running or not? I let my body make the decision and instead I watched football on Sky TV, relaxed and read the papers.

I didn't go for another run until Tuesday 25th October, which was fine because I was in the tapering off part of my training plan with less running and a couple of days off between runs.

I'd decided that Tuesday evening would be hill training again: four more laps of this gruelling hill. It felt great. I felt I had found a new angle for my training once more, and I realised during my third lap that it was only just over a week until we flew to New York.

I ordered a large four-wheeled case on the internet as I was working out how much luggage I would need. We were going for six nights, so I'd need a good selection of running clothing and then my normal clothes on top.

I took another day of rest followed by a six-mile run the following night. It was my regular 8.63-mile route cut short to six miles through being tired after yet another busy day at work. It wasn't really an issue though as I was probably doing a bit more than the recommended distances in the tapering process.

Saturday 29th October would be my last long run before the marathon. It should have been a twelve-miler but I chose to go for thirteen again as I felt so good. I'd had pasta on the Friday night, no alcohol, plenty of water, and even bought myself a new skin-tight breathable t-shirt that I could wear underneath my Nike royal blue running vest if the weather was cold, as it can be in New York in November.

I woke up at seven on Saturday 29th, had my jam on toast with a cup of tea followed by my sports hydration drink. As I sat at the breakfast bar sipping my tea, I watched the news and was horrified to see the news flash that New York was suffering really heavy snow.

Oh no, what was happening? Would it be cancelled? Surely I couldn't fail in two marathons!

I thought about this for a few moments but soon forced myself to move on to other thoughts, like my final run and getting everything right. After all, I didn't have much time to make sure I got my race right for next week.

I pressed the start button on my Garmin 305 watch as I left the house for my dress rehearsal long run.

I hit top form again with yet another PB of one hour, thirty-nine minutes and twenty-one seconds. I had broken the one hour forty barrier. I felt amazing that I was getting faster and faster.

Later that evening Lucy and I studied New York's nightlife and its restaurants and bars. We chatted about what we would both like to do in New York after the marathon; after all this was a holiday for us too. Then I reviewed my training plan and worked out that I had only three more runs to complete before getting on the plane to New York.

14 – One Week to Go

It was Monday 31st October. Today was my last hill training session, making a total of five over the last couple of weeks. Would that be enough to see me through?

My nerves were starting to kick in now whenever I thought about Sunday's race. I painted a picture in my mind about how everything was going to pan out. It looked good, although my nerves kept me awake each night or I'd wake at four in the morning full of questions. Was I ready? Had I done enough training? Well, it was too late for me to change anything now before taking to the stage in New York.

The heavy snow in New York was only affecting the suburbs now; I was hugely relieved that it was unlikely to affect the marathon in six days' time. I was monitoring the New York temperatures and they were very similar to the UK: a minimum of four degrees rising to twelve degrees each day. This was of course good news.

Tuesday 1st Nov was yet another busy day at work, followed by my penultimate run, a six-miler at a pace of 7.41 minutes a mile. I was pretty pleased with my pace; it remained consistent, but more importantly I felt relaxed at the same time.

We packed our suitcases on Wednesday night, before doing some more research on the New York sights. We were especially keen on seeing Ground Zero and the 9/11 Memorial.

Thursday 3rd November was a special day for me. It was my last day at work, and it was my last run before Sunday as we were flying to New York on Friday at twelve noon. I left my last run until as late as possible. Lucy and I were staying at a hotel at London Heathrow Airport overnight so we could relax and not have to worry about the M25 motorway traffic early on a busy Friday morning. This now meant my last run would be Thursday morning before work.

My alarm bleeped at half-five. I opened my eyes and clambered out of bed, before peering through the venetian blinds to see darkness and lots of fog.

I pulled on my running gear and left the house still half asleep, after stretching for a few minutes. I didn't start very well; my watch was bleeping reminding me that I was going too slow, much slower than recent weeks. I kept reminding myself that today was not a day to break records, it was just a slow, gentle pace. My chest felt a little tight. Was it just the nerves or the early morning start?

I finished my 8.63 favourite route with a time of an hour and nine minutes, a pace of 8.41, I felt disappointed that my final run was much slower than my recent performances, but I had to have a bad run at some point, didn't I? I would rather the bad run was today rather than Sunday after all, so I put it behind me, showered, had my bowl of cereal and went to work.

I arrived at the office and got stuck straight into work. I attended several meetings and eventually finished work at four, having made sure all my projects were complete and handed over.

I arrived home at 16:30hrs and relaxed with a cup of tea. Then I completed my packing, performing three checks that I had all of my running gear along with the accessories such as plasters, hydration tablets, safety pins and Vaseline. I was so paranoid that I decided to pack my trainers, shorts, vest, t-shirt and socks, watch and hydration tablets into my hand luggage in the unlikely event that my suitcase got lost in transit somehow. With all that had gone before, a little paranoia and even OCD was surely understandable…

15 – Overnight at Heathrow

We were staying at the Premier Inn hotel on Bath Road, close to Heathrow's Terminal 3, where we had to be by half eight on Friday morning. Lucy's parents arrived at our house to collect us and Lucy and I performed a last-minute check through our cases before leaving the house and locking up.

We finally set off. I nervously checked my running gear several times on the one-hour trip. I was feeling very low, tired and exhausted now that I had reached the last hurdle of my journey to New York.

We arrived at the hotel, a basic but decent enough hotel for a one-night stay. I was impressed though by the glass mezzanine area filled with gastro type restaurants and eateries, all very cool looking for a hotel like this.

It was half seven when we checked in and dropped the luggage off at the room. We went back to the glass mezzanine area to meet Den and Lyn for dinner in one of the gastro pubs. They'd be on their way for a weekend to the Cotswolds early on Friday, so they'd decided to stay over too.

I'd been eating healthy for the last month and wanted to continue. I looked through the menu and went for the hot salmon salad. It was an amazing dish and my plan to drink water only went out of the window immediately when I made the decision to have a glass or two of wine with the others. A couple of glasses of wine wouldn't hurt me after all of this training, and plenty of water between the wine was a good idea.

We finally left the restaurant at half eight for a good night's sleep, but the bed was hard and uncomfortable. Something was bothering me too, but I couldn't put my finger on it. I was tired and exhausted, and I woke several times during the night, my mind racing away.

16 – 4th Nov Virgin Flight VS021 to New York

My alarm went off at seven with a loud 'bleep bleep', I leapt out of bed and peered out of the window, to be greeted by a dark, miserable and wet London morning.

We showered, packed, left the hotel room and promptly checked out at half eight. We wandered out to the car park and packed our luggage into Den's car. Outside it was cold, dark and damp and the black London taxis were dashing up and down the dual carriageway outside the hotel like worker ants. Stop , start , turn left and right they went. We slowly weaved our way through the traffic with the rain pouring down. It was only a ten-minute journey but it seemed to take forever with the volume of traffic around the perimeter roads of the airport.

We arrived at the Terminal 3 drop-off point for departures and exchanged goodbyes with Den and Lynn. It was still pouring heavily as we dashed across the drop-off point to the T3 entrance, My mobile rang and rang in my pocket on vibrate but just as I managed to get my phone out of my pocket it stopped…a missed call and THEN a voicemail…

17 – A Devastating Blow to the Trip

Lucy and I were glad to be inside the terminal finally, away from the winter weather outside. We had arranged to meet Brian and his partner Sadie in the Virgin Atlantic Airways lounge at around 9:30am. Just before we went to the check-in area, I checked my mobile phone as I had just missed a call. The missed call number was my work number, and I racked my brains to work out if there was anything I'd left incomplete, or anyone I hadn't informed of my holiday plans.

And then I listened to the voicemail.

Oh my word... How can that be? I was in shock...

I ended the voicemail call and looked at Lucy; she looked back at me, concerned. I put my phone back in my pocket and explained the contents of the message. It was Brian's voice I'd heard, telling me that he and his partner had been ill throughout the night and were both too sick to travel until later on that day or perhaps tomorrow...

Why? How? What? My mind spat out a stream of questions I couldn't answer.

We proceeded to check-in, both in shock that Brian and Sadie would not be travelling with us. We took the elevator towards the Virgin Upper Class lounge and I purchased some US dollars at the bureau de change kiosk, still not thinking straight at this point. I called Brian to see how he was feeling and what his plans were but there was no reply, so I left a voicemail sharing our disappointment that he was too sick to travel. I knew exactly how he would be feeling right now as I had been through the same only a handful of months before.

The sad possibility was that Brian potentially would NOT be running the New York City Marathon. I checked the schedules and found that there three more Virgin flights to New York throughout the day that would enable Brian to get there in time to run the marathon. Will they be on the later flight, I wondered? What would I do if I felt like that?

We wandered through to the lounge, still feeling confused about the absence of Brian and Sadie. We found ourselves a nice quiet comfy area in the Virgin Upper Class Clubhouse. The lounge itself was very cool and had a chilled out vibe. It was around ten o'clock as we relaxed in the black leather swivel chairs overlooking the runway, the smell of breakfast wafting in our direction. A smartly dressed and polite waiter asked what we would like to order from the breakfast menu. I chose the eggs Benedict on a wholemeal bagel, a fairly healthy option with good protein. Lucy went for poached eggs with a glass of champagne to calm her nerves as she doesn't really enjoy flying and also just because she could have a glass of champagne at 10:30 on a Friday morning... I declined the champagne as I had had one of my 'sins' last night: those couple of glasses of wine with dinner. All of the holding back would be over in just two days.

I wandered around the Clubhouse lounge and saw several marathon runners in their sports attire. I preferred not to appear so obvious, travelling in smart jeans with a smart shirt rather than the brightly coloured tracksuits worn by some of the runners I spotted around us.

Our breakfast arrived within ten minutes of ordering. It was amazingly good, and we followed it up with tea and regular glasses of water. We continued to relax and read the daily newspapers and watch the planes take off..

At around 11am a final call was announced for the passengers travelling to New York on flight VS021 to make their way to departure gate 20. We left the clubhouse and made our way to the departure gates. As we approached the gate a Virgin ground staff attendant informed us that the incoming flight had been delayed by approximately an hour. After around thirty minutes of waiting the queues began to move and we were boarding, albeit a little later than expected.

We walked up to the entrance of the plane and were greeted by two happy, smiling faces and the bright red suits of Virgin Atlantic. Lucy and I were shown to our seats, and then promptly offered a glass of champagne. Once again I thought briefly I shouldn't be drinking alcohol yet again.

This book may sound like I am some kind of alcoholic, but I'm honestly not! That said, I made the decision to accept the complimentary champagne. It went down so well that I slumped back in my seat and accepted another glass before we took off.

I was feeling really good, the bubbles of the champagne had gone straight to my head. I glanced to my left where Brian and Sadie would have been sitting. Would they be on the next flight or the later evening flight? I wouldn't know for the next seven hours while we crossed the Atlantic. I realised that if Brian did not make the flight at some point on Friday then he wouldn't be able to take part at all; registration was the following day between nine and five, and you have to collect your running number in person.

I sat back in my seat and thought how lucky I was and really felt for Brian, who at this stage looked like he was not going to make the race.

Soon after 13:20 we were airborne, the rain pouring down and the skies cloudy and grey outside. The flight was bumpy from shortly after takeoff until we moved above the low-lying clouds.

When lunch was served, I opted for the healthy chicken risotto and Lucy picked the Thai chicken noodles followed by the healthy fruit option. It was now time to relax on the full flatbed and watch a film so I could get as much rest as possible before the race. I actually dozed off, missing the first half an hour of The Hangover Part II. I might not have seen the set-up, but the rest of the film kept me amused, and I felt distinctly refreshed.

Eventually the pilot announced on the tannoy that we would be landing in approximately forty minutes. I looked out of the window; it was bright and sunny, yet looked bitterly cold. There were traces of snow on the buildings and snow covered the fields below. It appeared that snow was still affecting the outer suburbs of New York and not Manhattan, I hoped.

As the landing gear sounded I wondered again if Brian had made one of the later flights...

18 – Arrival at JFK Airport

Sssssccccccccccccccrrrrrrrrrrrrrrrreeeeeeeeecccccccccchhhhhhhhh…

The wheels of the Boeing 747 touched down on the sun-drenched runway of John F Kennedy Airport in New York at four thirty, just before the sun set behind the city skyline.

We taxied along the runway and finally arrived at stand K30, the engines were cut and then the silence of the aircraft could be heard, passengers jumped up excitedly from their seats and opening the overhead luggage compartments. Everybody claimed their baggage and finally the impatient air dispersed with a burst of energy as we were allowed to disembark and make the short walk into the arrivals hall.

The weather looked unexpectedly mild for this time of the year in New York although we hadn't felt the outdoor temperatures yet. As we strolled into the customs and security hall, we were greeted with about ten lines of passengers waiting to be allowed into the US after waiting patiently for thirty minutes. We were questioned why we were in New York, how long we were staying, where we were staying, had our fingerprints and photos taken and our passports checked.

I looked around the airport and spotted lots of marathon runners, it seemed a popular time to arrive ahead of Sunday's big race.

As the carousel of the baggage reclaim started to move, I made a mental note to be careful of doing anything that might cause an injury, like lifting our suitcases from the carousel and injuring my back… Fortunately a baggage attendant was removing the luggage from the carousel to save the passengers the heavy work. We identified our luggage and headed for the exit and taxi signs.

As we stepped outside, we saw a huge queue for the taxis and opted instead for the shuttle bus that went direct to Grand Central Station. It was Friday rush hour, so we expected there to be a fair amount of traffic into Manhattan. We paid $32 for two single tickets that would take us to within a five-minute walk of our hotel in Times Square.

We waited outside in the dark until the shuttle bus arrived. There was a cold chill in the air; in the space of just an hour the temperature had dropped to what felt like five or six degrees.

We placed our luggage at the back of the shuttle bus before climbing aboard. It wasn't much warmer on the bus as there were windows that were wedged open or broken, and music was blaring from the speakers.
We finally left JFK at around six forty-five and travelled along several freeways before coming to a halt in the rush hour traffic. The shuttle bus moved along slowly in the bus lane, before entering the Queens-Midtown Tunnel that crosses beneath the East River and taking us on to Manhattan.

Finally I had arrived in the city that holds the largest marathon in the world.

The shuttle bus pulled to a sudden halt. We had arrived at Grand Central Station, where this bus terminated. We were reunited with our luggage once again and I checked my iPhone for the directions to our hotel.

Looking up, I could see bright lights everywhere, advertising boards, theatre lights and more. This city was buzzing and the cost of its electricity didn't bear thinking about. No chance of New York becoming a green city anytime soon.

The cold air had now turned distinctly bitter and the wind bit at our faces as we walked the three blocks to the hotel on 45th Street on 6th Avenue.

=

We entered the revolving doors of the Marriott Marquis Hotel and took the elevator up to the hotel lobby on the eighth floor. The marble floor gave me a warm feeling that the hotel would be great quality, but we were both shattered.

I walked up to the desk, provided my booking reference and within thirty seconds had been given my room key for the next six nights.

"There you go sir, room 3320, have a nice stay." It was said in a very friendly American voice..

We took the elevator to the thirty-third floor and entered the spacious room and were greeted with floor to ceiling views of those bright flashing lights of Times Square. At last.

We were exhausted after a long day spent travelling, but my mind was still very much awake with so much to think about before Sunday's race. I drew the curtains on that incredible view, to a feeling of stillness and to finally signal the end of a long day.

19 – Saturday 5th November 2011

My alarm bleeped loudly at half seven. Only twenty-four hours before the New York City Marathon, one of the many biggest days of my life.

The jet lag from that four-hour time difference and the disruptive day of travelling was just starting to attack me as I sat in bed reminding myself where I was. Today I had to visit the Jakob E Kravitz Convention Center on 2nd Avenue and 42nd Street to collect my running number and official ING-sponsored running bag.

I was feeling peckish so I put some clothes on and went down to the eighth floor to grab some breakfast from Starbucks.

I saw several tens of runners all gearing up for a final run before Sunday. I'd had my last run on Thursday morning, and even though it felt a long time ago now, I knew my mind felt right at this point. There was no urge to go for a run. I bought some yoghurt and muesli for a healthy breakfast and returning to the room. Lucy hadn't fully woken, so didn't want anything to eat just yet.

I sat on the sofa and watched the local US TV channels, pleased to hear that Sunday's weather was to be around ten degrees and sunny, just about perfect weather for running a marathon.

I opened the curtains to reveal the New York skyline. The bright flashing lights of Times Square from last night were gone, but the city still looked very 3D as I gazed out through those magnificent floor to ceiling windows. I finished off my healthy berry flavoured yoghurt and muesli and took a shower. Lucy was awake now, ready for a day of exploring this exciting city.

Within forty-five minutes we were ready to head off to the convention centre to collect my race number. Lucy promptly reminded me to take my passport as proof of ID, something that all runners had to take in exchange of their running number. No passport, no race number.

We left the room and walked towards the elevator along the hotel hallways. The atrium below was filled voices, loud, cheering, shouting, and laughing. Downstairs on the ground floor there were a few hundred runners waiting to take part in the Dash to the Finish 5k run that was to be held in Central Park as a warm-up. I'd chosen not to take part as I knew that I had trained to the correct level and I was ready to run on Sunday and not before.

We stepped out into bright sunshine and a bitter cold wind. I sipped on the cold bottle of water that I'd resolved to take throughout the day to remain hydrated. Within ten minutes I had to find somewhere to go to the toilet, thanks to a combination of taking on so much water, the cold weather and being nervous about the race. It's a little-known fact that cold weather has a habit of making people want to go for a pee!

We walked down 45th Street to 2nd Avenue and then turned left and walked four blocks to 49th Street. It was a fresh brisk walk, and really nice to see some of the back streets of New York in daylight. There wasn't a cloud in that amazing bright blue sky, but it was only around five degrees. I couldn't help but think ahead to this time tomorrow.

Shortly after arriving at the convention centre, I found myself nearly running to the toilets again. That was twice in twenty minutes; it must be down to nerves, surely? I continued to sip my water and polished off a breakfast snack bar. We walked to the registration entrance, where we were greeted by very enthusiastic American ING marathon officials dressed in the orange sponsored ING t-shirts, saying "Hey you guys, good luck for the race" and "Have a great day, enjoy and smile!"

I felt special and honoured to be taking part in the biggest race in the world.

I found my race number collection point of 40,000 – 41,000, produced my passport and letter of authorisation and in exchange received my running number and a clear plastic UPS clothes bag with lots of freebies inside.

I looked around everywhere; the convention centre was buzzing with what felt to me a nervous energy and people were buying lots of official merchandise. We wandered through the ASICS clothing area where I decided to buy a long sleeved white t-shirt with the slogan *To Hell and Back* emblazoned across its back, a reference to the gruelling New York City Marathon.

After purchasing my official merchandise, I bought five cereal bars of various flavours - chocolate berry, peanut butter, cookies 'n cream - to fuel my body for the rest of the day and before the race tomorrow. After an hour of wandering around we both decided we had seen enough. There were too many people bumping into each other and it was getting quite stuffy in the convention centre with the sheer volume of people. So it was time to depart back downtown to Times Square, with another swift trip to the gents. We dropped my race number and bag off at the hotel and headed into Times Square.

Saturday was to be a relaxing day, with not too much walking and sightseeing; I didn't want to be tired by the start of the race. Lucy suggested we go to the theatre, so we found the infamous half-price theatre ticket office booth in Times Square, queued up and managed to score a couple of half-price matinee tickets for Sister Act, based on the Whoopi Goldberg film. The show started at 2pm on Broadway and 59th Street, only a ten-minute walk up Broadway, so there was just enough time for a healthy lunch at a local deli.

At just after one we found a typical American deli where we both chose a grilled chicken, pesto, cheese and tomato panini, which I washed down with yet more water. The atmosphere was really buzzing and we could hear lots of chatting about marathon times at every table. It was marathon mania everywhere in New York.

After finishing the Panini's we settled the bill and left for the theatre. We strolled up to 59th Street in the bright sunshine and were greeted by a long queue that stretched around the corner of the theatre. It was bitterly cold, we were in the shade and the wind chill wasn't in our favour. After a five-minute wait, the queue moved along the pavement and we were standing beneath the striking black, white and purple and huge Sister Act billboard that could be seen all the way down Broadway.

I could just about see the start of Central Park in the distance and, if I remembered rightly, I reckoned I'd have this sight tomorrow at mile 24 as I turned into the park for the most gruelling part of the race..

...and back to reality, where lots of traditional yellow taxis lined up at the traffic lights of 59th and Broadway, steam seeped out of the manhole covers in the street, and sirens sounded in the distance; this was the New York we all know and love from countless movies and TV shows.

As we waited patiently I received an SMS message from Brian wishing me good luck for Sunday, and confirming that he would not be able to make it... Lucy and I were devastated for him, but I knew I had to put that to the back of my mind, and remain positive.

The queue continued moving towards the wooden doors with their big gold door handles. We could hear many conversations all around us and it seemed just about everybody in New York was here to take part in the marathon. We wandered past the security doorman and upstairs to the dress circle where we took our seats.

FFFFrrrrrrrrreezing cold. It was absolutely freezing in this theatre. I'm sure it was colder in the theatre than outside, and we kept our coats and scarves wrapped tight around us as we waited in anticipation for the start of the show.

The curtain came up shortly after two, with high energy gospel music from the start. The song *Take Me to Heaven* remained in my head throughout the show. It was a perfect way to pass the time before the big race, a great way to relax, unwind and just enjoy myself.

The show finished just after 4.30pm, we walked outside to see the sun descending behind the tall buildings and the wind growing stronger. The forecast for tomorrow had changed to seven degrees and sunny; just about perfect running conditions. I certainly wouldn't be dripping with sweat. We returned to the hotel and relaxed by watching TV for a couple of hours. I continued to drink my water and ate another cereal bar.

I also needed this time to try my running gear on and make sure I had everything. I pinned my race number on my vest, adjusted everything so the whole outfit was perfect and then went through 20 minutes of stretching. I checked my bag, then checked my bag again and again three more times. I was happy now.

Hmm, more water. I felt like I had drunk the Atlantic Ocean.

It was now 6.30pm. I felt right inside, mentally, emotionally. This was so important: the marathon is a mental endurance almost as much as it is a physical one. I was ready in all areas, mentally, physically and now I knew my running gear was perfect. All I had to worry about now was the clock change at two in the morning. The East Coast would be going back an hour, as if the runners need another thing to think about!

I set two alarms on my mobile phone, the hotel's automated alarm call and Lucy's mobile for 4:30am. It was a really early start and it would feel like the middle of the night, especially now that my jetlag was really kicking in now.

At this point I thought I could relax, so we showered, changed and left the hotel room for an early dinner at half seven. We both agreed this would the last night of being quite so sensible. Lucy had supported me throughout the last month of healthy eating and drinking very little alcohol. That last 10K race in sweltering conditions and the alcohol-fuelled family BBQ that followed it were nearly seven weeks ago.

My mind wandered a little; I'd soon be taking on the challenge I'd intended to complete six months ago. The time had nearly arrived for me to take the dramatic stage of the Verrazano-Narrows Bridge.

We walked just a few minutes from Times Square as it was so bitterly cold. the wind scratching at my face. We found a restaurant called BOND45. It was typically American, and served pasta, steak and seafood, all with an Italian twist. The antipasto at the entrance was on full view as we walked in, an amazing array of colours, nicely presented on oversized white square plates. We gave our names to the maitre d' and were offered a seat at the bar while our table was being prepared.

The bar area was very dark with low lighting, lots of mirrors and black and white photos of famous people adorning the restaurant walls. We both loved the look and feel of the place.

Lucy ordered a large glass of Sauvignon Blanc, while I ordered a large diet coke. The barman commented, "Not another person running the marathon?" to which I replied "Yes, I am afraid so".

I certainly wasn't the only runner in the place. Around us were various groups of people, all sporting newly purchased official ING marathon clothing and all eating large bowls of pasta.

Now, traditionally pasta is thought to fuel the muscles and top up glycogen levels for energy, however some folk will say NOT to eat pasta the night before a race as it simply will not make a difference.

Another ten minutes later we were shown to our table on the mezzanine level, where we had a really good view of the restaurant. I chose a bowl of pasta to keep the tradition going and ordered another diet coke. This was definitely going to be my last night of being good for a long time.

The food turned out to be very average - great presentation but lacking in quality. Deep down in my mind, I was just wishing the evening away to focus on Sunday. That's quite sad really as the trip to New York was a holiday after tomorrow afternoon, and there's me wishing away my second night of the seven-night trip.

Lucy had ordered beef sliders which were like mini-burgers, but sadly virtually cremated and the beef tough and chewy. We mentioned it to the waitress, who then kindly brought a huge slice of New York cheesecake by way of an apology – or perhaps to ensure her 18-20% gratuity tip. We laughed and discussed this topic throughout the trip, debating whether this is a fair deal to the paying customer. But it's a cultural thing in the US; bar and waiting staff rely heavily on customer's tips, whereas in the UK you usually give up to 10%, and more if you have received good food and service.

We thanked her for the cheesecake; I had eaten enough food for the night to keep me fuelled until Sunday morning, but hadn't overindulged. We left the restaurant at around nine and were back relaxing in the hotel room just before half past.

It was nearly time for bed as it was such an early start the next day. We watching a little TV and chatted about tomorrow and where Lucy was going to see me in the race... well, more like *hope* to see me.

I completed one more check of my running gear, which I'd left laid out on the sofa. The weather caused me a little uncertainty. Would it be so cold that I'd have to wear a t-shirt under my vest? That set off further questions: what time should I eat in the morning? Will that be enough food before the race?

My Gel Kayano 17 trainers had about 100 miles of pounding the streets, so they were worn in and ready

My ASICS socks had been worn once, about two weeks ago when I ran my eighteen-mile run, so I knew they wouldn't rub.

My grey Nike running shorts with blue and white trim had been worn for the last month along with a pair of navy blue cycling shorts that I always wore to avoid chaffing at the top of my legs where my shorts would otherwise rub.

My only concern was the weather. Should I wear my breathable white tight t-shirt to keep warm underneath my royal blue Nike running vest or do I go without? And why was I struggling to make a simple decision?

I finally switched the lights out at ten past ten after a final check that the four alarms remained set to go off at half four the following morning. The final worry of the night was the clocks going back one hour. But on the plus side, at least if there was a problem with the clock or mobile phones I would be awake at half three - an hour early rather than the other way round. So there was no way I would miss the marathon.

ZZZZZZZZZ....

I woke up once during the night at seven minutes past two precisely, but soon returned to a deep sleep.

20 – The Big Day – Sunday 6th November

Bleep, bleep, bleep… it was 4:30am on Sunday 6th November and three alarms were telling me my moment had finally arrived.

I slowly opened my eyes, switched on the bedside table lamp, and lay still in the dimly lit room. I took a minute to repeat to myself the mantra "today is going to be a good day." Already I could feel the adrenalin trickling through my body.

I got up, showered and then made myself cup of sweet tea. I sat on the sofa, taking everything in. I found myself staring at the wall and slowing right down, returning to stillness in my mind. Lucy was half-awake and we chatted about very basic things like the sights I was going to see and how I should simply enjoy the race. This really helped me to put everything into perspective.

I wasn't hungry, so I didn't eat. My theory is that you should eat before a big race if you feel like it, not just because the text books tell you to. I drank plenty of water, although I was careful not to take on too much after my experiences the previous day. I didn't want to get caught short on the coach to Staten Island.

Time was ticking. It was five past five and I had to meet the Sports International tour group and fellow runners at half five in the hotel lobby.

I slowly put my running gear on, checking each item carefully, including Compeed plasters to prevent any unwanted blisters on my heels, the Vaseline around my nipples to avoid any painful chaffing and bleeding. I zipped up the adidas hoodie I'd brought to keep me warm while standing around and my adidas royal blue windcheater waterproof jacket in case it rained, before finally pulling on my frankly unflattering adidas navy blue running tights,. They weren't pretty but they'd keep me warm. Finally I pulled on my trainers and tied them very loosely.

It was now twenty past five and time for me to say goodbye to Lucy. She wished me all the luck in the world, we hugged and kissed and exchanged a few personal and meaningful words.

I left the hotel room at 5:23am with everything I needed to complete the New York City Marathon in under four hours.

I walked out of the hotel's elevator into the lobby, turned the corner and found the bright blue running jackets of Sports International Tours dotted around everywhere. I found who I thought was the organiser, Karen, and introduced myself, as I had had a brief telephone conversation with her the previous day about Brian being unable to make the trip due to his illness.

I exchanged a few brief hellos with fellow runners while we waited to leave. It was still very early, so not really a good time for big and deep conversations and after all we were English and too polite to be brash, loud or probing at such an early hour.

Shortly after half five our group of twenty or thirty runners walked the short distance to the New York Library on 42nd Street. It was dry but freezing cold, about two degrees, and very dark on the quiet streets of New York

As we walked along I chatted to Karen about her previous trips to New York. She had organised the last five annual trips to New York, was from Blackpool in the north of England, and she made me feel very welcome. She asked me if I'd run the New York race before and what time I was hoping for – what seemed to be everybody's first and second questions when chatting about marathons. I explained that it was my first overseas marathon and that I was looking at anything under four hours.

Secretly of course I wanted to be much better than that, but after hearing a lot of people say that in New York you should add an extra fifteen minutes onto your predicted time because of the bridges and the steep inclines leading up to them, I decided to settle for anything under four hours. Even 3:59:59 would be amazing.

As we neared the New York Library I got chatting to a guy named Kevin from Newcastle, or Redcar I think. Somewhere in the northeast of England anyway. He had run this marathon in 2010 so I was able to throw a few open questions about various topics, to ease my nervous tension about the race.

We queued up outside the library and were asked to show our running numbers as proof we were running. We shuffled along and turned the corner before being confronted with twenty or thirty silver Greyhound buses, all ready to take the herds of runners to the starting line at Staten Island. Kevin and I boarded the next available coach and continued to chat casually about past marathons and previous finish times, as marathon runners do. Kevin was of a similar standard to me, with probably a few more marathons under his belt than my two.

The atmosphere on the bus was fairly sombre; pockets of conversations broke out here and there. For some runners it was their tenth, twentieth or thirtieth New York marathon, while for some it was their first ever marathon race. You could actually hear the worry and fear in their voices after hearing the stories from the more experienced.
Six o'clock passed as I looked out of the bus window into the bitter cold, and I felt my first hunger pain. I had my food supplies in my UPS clothing bag but decided not to eat anything until we had arrived As we motored from one freeway to another on the bus journey to Staten Island, Kevin shared with me his previous marathon experiences including the New York marathon in 2010.

We crossed bridges and went through tunnels and along more freeways before approaching the famous Verrazano-Narrows Bridge, a two-tiered suspension bridge more than two and a half miles long. It was a simply incredible piece of engineering. To my surprise Kevin explained that we would be running over this bridge as it's where the race starts. Oh my God! This bridge was huge. I was stunned after seeing the incline as the bus struggled on the approach. Sunrise was not far away now, the dark skies turning a grey-blue colour with the sun trying to escape the darkness in the distance.

As we crossed the bridge I glanced down to my right and saw a large cruise ship moving slowly towards Manhattan. It was one of the Celebrity Cruises fleet and the ship was called *Eclipse*. This was the very same ship that Lucy and I had sailed on earlier in the year from Miami to the Caribbean! How spooky that I should see the exact ship that I had been on - my first and only cruise ship seen again on my first New York marathon.

As we reached the end of the Verrazano-Narrows Bridge, my new mate Kevin explained that we would be dropped off and left to camp here for the next three hours or so.

It was now about half six and the sun was starting to rise as I stepped off the coach. Brrrrrrr, it was bitter, about zero degrees, and I was grateful for my layers of clothing to keep me warm. There were hundreds of fellow runners wherever I looked, and we followed the crowds down a wide pathway lined by private marquees and tents (these were for the elite runners) until we reached the interchange of posts for the three differently-coloured start points: green, orange and blue.

We were both in the green start area; I was in starting corral 40 and starting the marathon at ten past ten, Kevin in corral 19 and starting at nine forty. The corrals are the starting pens or enclosures that you line up in prior to the start of the race. I was unaware until I chatted with Kevin that there were three different start times at the New York City Marathon, known as waves. Wave 1 was at nine forty for the elite and faster runners, wave 2 at ten past ten for the medium performance runners and wave 3 at ten forty was for the slower runners.

As we continued to the green start area I could see and hear live bands on stages, rock music blaring out on the main stage, followed by some jazz music on another stage. I followed Kevin as he knew where he was going, and soon I saw the signs for the green start. There were hundreds of blue plastic portaloos near the corrals, which I was pretty sure would be very busy in the next two hours or so.

Lots of people had already arrived, and some were in sleeping bags to stay warm on this bitterly cold Sunday morning. A light south-easterly wind bit into my face as Kevin and I wandered around the food and drink stalls to see what it was all about. Complementary snacks and beverages, from tea, coffee and breakfast cereal bars to Lucozade and bagels. I grabbed myself a milky coffee with extra sugar from Dunkin' Donuts and a couple of breakfast bars to add to the collection I'd purchased the previous day.

We found a spot in the middle of the green start area so we could see everything, fairly central to all of the amenities, including the giant screen providing details of the baggage drop and the corral start times. We stood rather than sat, just to make sure we stayed warm on this freezing cold morning. I performed a few stretches so that my body didn't seize up. I had just less than three hours before my ten past ten start time. The reason for the painfully early arrival was the Verrazano-Narrows Bridge itself; as the starting point for the race it needed to be closed at seven to prepare for the start. So all runners had to be at the start by half six at the latest.

I pulled a sports drink out of my bag and sipped frequently, followed by a breakfast bar as I had a few hunger pains just creeping in. I ate little and often as the experts recommend. As I chewed on my breakfast bar, I turned around and took in the atmosphere and the amazing view of the bridge. The sun was shining, not a cloud in the sky, and this huge steel monster loomed against the bright blue skyline, the sun rays creeping through the steel girders. It was simply enormous, and I'd soon be running across it.

It was now half seven, and people everywhere were making themselves comfortable on the grass, some in sleeping bags and others with all-in-one body suits to keep out the biting wind blowing from the east. It was still only about four or five degrees, but with that clear sky and bright sun it was shaping up to be perfect marathon running weather. The queues at the portaloos were steadily growing as the thousands of runners were starting to become nervous after taking on board both food and drinks. There were officials handing out bagels and bottle of water, the hospitality was amazing, even better than the London Marathon. The music from the stage continued to thud away in the distance between the green and orange start areas, it felt like I was at a music festival rather than a marathon.

I had my next food parcel about forty-five minutes after my first breakfast bar. It was a healthy chicken salad sandwich that I had bought from a deli just before it closed yesterday evening; it was the right amount to keep me satisfied without feeling full. I continued sipping slowly on my orange-flavoured sports drink to keep myself hydrated.

I carried out a few more light stretches and thought about my race tactics. Was I ready? Was I fit enough? What about any niggling injuries, or setting off too fast or too slow? There were so many correct decisions I had to make to ensure I'd have a good run.

The mass of dark armoured-looking UPS baggage trucks stood side by side in a long line waiting for the first herd of excited runners to drop off their belongings before heading off to the starting corrals. The first tannoy for the green start runners was only a few minutes away now... It was just after eight, the sun was rising in the sky and the temperature following it upwards very so slowly, but still there was this cold, biting wind cutting through the runners.

There were three starts at the New York marathon, to allow 47,000 runners a fair and equal start. These are divided by three different start locations - green, blue and orange - all very close to each other, but far enough apart to avoid congestion. The corrals for each colour had further numbering based on the runners' predicted finish time on application. My official running number was 40,255. This meant I was the 255th person in corral 40, where each corral could hold around 2,000 people.

Roughly thirty to forty-five minutes before your scheduled race start you are called to your numbered corral. Before you go into the corral you need to remove the warm layers of clothing, place them in your clothing bag and drop that off at the numbered UPS trucks These trucks would make the journey to Central Park to wait for you to finish the race. An impressively neat and efficient process. What a long way off that was though, I was thinking to myself. In around four hours' time my dream of running New York would be complete and not a nightmare!

Hopefully, if I ran my race correctly and put everything I had learnt in the last six months into practice, I would be celebrating.

21 - Final Moments before the Start

The time seemed to be going quite quickly now and it was fast approaching half past eight. Another degree on the thermometer, a few more rays of sun... It was now eight degrees.

Kevin was in wave 1, so he'd be leaving soon. The atmosphere was hotting up, and the activity levels increased, with lots of people walking in different directions, heading to and from the toilets, eating, drinking, queuing at the UPS trucks to drop baggage off.

I had my last breakfast bar and continued sipping on my sports drink. I had eaten three times so far, at half six, half seven and half eight. I felt good, only eating when I felt like it rather than sticking to advice meted out by a marathon book.

Kevin and I exchanged a good luck handshake and off he went. It was now 8:45am and now that I was on my own it was time to get my head in the right place, get my body stretched to its maximum to produce the performance of my life. Was this to be the day I triumphed in a marathon in less than four hours? I had only run two previous marathons, both in London. I'd completed my first in four hours and eighteen minutes, the second in four hours and five minutes, so this could be a case of third time lucky.

My god, I was beginning to feel a little weird right now. My nerves began to kick in as it was only an hour or so until I'd hear *New York New York* booming through the big speakers at the bridge.

I went for my first of many visits to the portaloo, waiting patiently in the orderly queues enforced by the security officials.

I found a spot on the grass bank in the sun to ensure that I stayed warm before the race. There I performed a good fifteen minutes of stretching, taking each stretch very slowly to make sure I didn't overstretch or tweak any cold muscles. This final warm-up was so vital as it was the last chance to really get into 'the running zone'. There were fewer runners around now as the final call for all runners for the wave 1 start could be heard. A further final call was made to all wave 1 runners: CLOSED...

Having completed my stretching routines and warmed myself, I left it as late as possible before peeling off my navy adidas running tights and blue adidas waterproof jacket. I checked my running number was fastened securely and applied two big lumps of Vaseline to my nipples to stop any bleeding or chafing. I removed my adidas hoodie and felt the cold chill across the back of my neck.

I performed a few more stretches and paid two more visits to the portaloos; I had to get rid of some of this sports drink I had been consuming for the last 3 hours.

I felt nervous now. Really nervous.

The tannoy announced that it was ten minutes until the wave 2 runners could go to the corrals. I made my way to the UPS trucks to drop my clothing bag off. As I stood in the queue I thought what an amazing job the marathon officials do of organising 47,000 bags and transporting them to the finish line in Central Park. I seemed to be having quite a few of these odd thoughts now, nervous energy I think.

Just before handing my bag to the officials I found my old black t-shirt to keep warm for the forty-five minutes until the start. I'd simply peel it off and then throw it, to be collected for charity. Instead of wearing a belt, which I'd found uncomfortable on previous marathons, I used safety pins to pin my four Lucozade Carbo Gels onto the inside top of my shorts, in line with my hips., where I wouldn't feel them as I ran. I dropped one of my hydration tablets into a bottle of water and put the others into a small plastic container that fit in the inside pocket in my shorts.

Having dropped my bag off at the UPS trucks, everything was complete and I was as ready as ever I could be.

A wave of excitement passed through me. I was so nervous, yet so excited to start the world-famous New York City Marathon. This really was a dream come true for me.

22 – The Corrals

I made my way to the starting corrals with the rest of the wave 2 runners, continuing to sip on my hydration drink as I.

Once I'd arrived, I could see thousands of runners making their way onto the huge Verrazano-Narrows Bridge. In the distance I could hear the sound of a female singer, followed by the Frank Sinatra classic *New York New York*, followed by the starting gun.

The 2011 marathon had started.

The crowds around me were very noisy with excitement. I took everything in, stood still and tilted my head backwards and closed my eyes, I stopped and allowed my mind to return to stillness. This was a way for me to relax and meditate, to get into the zone. Most marathons runners will do the same.

After three or four minutes I opened my eyes and made my way to another set of portaloos that were conveniently located in the corrals. I paid three more visits to the smelly portaloos in the next ten minutes.

Surely we would be moving to the start soon… Ten minutes, five minutes, and at last, the runners ahead of me shuffled forwards. The officials were asking the runners to remove any unnecessary clothing which could be collected and pass onto charity. Another great idea.

I removed the black t-shirt that I had been wearing to keep warm, leaving in my final running kit: my ASICS Gel Kayano 17s, white ClimaCool t-shirt underneath my royal blue Nike running vest and my running gloves. I'd simply throw the gloves away if I didn't need them during the race. I made my final trip to the portaloo before the race start. I counted ten trips in total.

Was that normal for runners or was I just really nervous?

We moved through the final section of the corral as the time approached ten o'clock. We turned left up on the concourse to the lower level of the bridge. My final check was that my Garmin 305 watch was switched on and all set. I had my watch set for eight-minute miles so it bleeped 'slow down' if I was under eight-minute miles and bleeped 'speed up' if I strayed over a nine-minute mile pace. I checked the GPS was active and the battery was full. I set my watch display to show time, distance, and current pace.

I was totally ready.

We turned the corner onto the lower level of the bridge. It was like waiting to go into a tunnel, the lower part of the bridge looking dark and cold as the sun was only warming the upper level. I waited patiently with the rest of the crowds, moving as far forward as possible. The crowds of runners were so colourful, people from all over the world displaying their national colours on their running clothing and charity vests. Some runners were still throwing their 'keeping warm' clothing to the side of the road, leaving it as late as possible in these fresh conditions.

The moment had arrived. It was 10:05, the sun was shining and while it was warming up, it was still very cold.

I looked around at the other runners and said "Good luck" to a couple nearby who were from France, just two of so many French runners in the race today.

A helicopter was hovering above, filming the wave 2 start. This momentous event was being shown around the world.

Over the tannoy a female voice began singing what sounded like the US national anthem. I stood still, a lump in my throat for what I was about to do. I was so proud to be running this race.

The next few minutes were amazing. I had a tear in my eye as I heard the sound of *New York New York* bellowing out through the speakers, making everybody smile and putting an extra yard in everybody's step; at least, it did mine.

23 – The Race Begins At 10:10

The 2011 marathon had finally begun for me. The first few runners sped across the start line, the runners in front of me moving fairly quickly, although crowded closely together.

I crossed the start line, pressed the start button on my Garmin 305 watch, and I was off.

I felt so excited, my heart racing and nerves tingling. It went dark in the enclosed part of the bridge. The incline here would be a sharp shock to some of the less fit runners, but I was hopeful that my training would show what I could do on this challenging course.

I started at a pace of eight minutes thirty seconds, although it felt like everybody was in my way. As most runners know, the basic rules say don't try to zigzag or weave your way through, so it was like running through an overcrowded train. I really couldn't get going, and I thought that perhaps lots of runners had put their predicted times down as much quicker than they were running. I had to find a way around the swarm of runners as this stretch across the water was two and a half miles wide. I decided to run on the kerb side that was narrow. It was high risk if I slipped, but it was my first decision of the race that paid off, otherwise I would have been running nine-minute miles for the first three miles.

I knew the pace I had to maintain to reach the finish time that I was aiming for, and it certainly wasn't nine minutes a mile.

I slipped into my zone after the first mile, comfortable now that I was passing the masses. I glanced to the left and saw the amazing views of the city and the skyline in the distance, the large mass of water, bright blue sky, and thought about the finish line in Manhattan that was waiting for me.

I concentrated on my feet right now, making sure I stayed on the narrow kerb. It was a good solution to get me back on track after the frustrating start. I opened my legs and increased my pace to 7.30 minutes a mile for the next mile and a half before I saw daylight and bright sunshine up ahead and the downhill section that was the exit from the bridge.

Here was the first opportunity since the start that a toilet stop could be had. The nerves that had been stored for the first two and a half miles were about to be released for the last time.

There must have been more than two hundred male runners lined up against what looked like a motorway bridge, where the light-coloured concrete was getting soaked with urinate. There were even two female runners that managed to urinate crouched down behind a pylon. It seems that anything goes in these situations. I returned to the road and picked up my pace again now that I was feeling refreshed.

There were a few supporters cheering us on even at this early stage on the outskirts of Brooklyn. It looked like we were running on a dual carriageway, and then the road went through a residential area. We turned left and then right, past houses built in a Victorian style, yet the brickwork looked about twenty years old.

We turned right and met the orange and blue start runners so we merged into one big race on the wide streets.

I breezed past mile three with a pace of 7.13 minutes a mile. I felt strong and in the zone.

The road bent round to the right and then opened out so I could see dead ahead for perhaps three or four miles. There were brightly coloured runners as far into the distance as I could see.

The atmosphere was magical; I'd loved every minute of the race so far.

I took my first liquid at a drinks station at mile four, a choice of green Gatorade or water. The only issue for me was that it was served in paper cups and not plastic bottles of water. This made drinking on the run a little more challenging without spilling it over my face, unless of course I slowed right down to a walking pace, which I wasn't about to do.

It took me a few attempts to master the art of drinking on the run with a paper cup. I clocked another 7.40 minute mile for mile five, so I was really pleased with my pace. The terrain was pretty flat and every so often I would have to weave my way through big groups of runners, who were happy to spread across the entire width of the road - maybe four or five people wide so i couldn't easily pass them. It angered me several times, so I would run past them and then slow down in front of them to make a point. But they were oblivious to my actions and I stopped playing this game after mile six as it was only going to waste my energy. It was just a case of runners who'd registered faster predicted finish times than their ability allowed.

This part of the race was a really comfortable time for me to review my pace and to make sure that I wasn't overachieving too early in the race. I glanced down at my watch almost continuously; I was still going well at 7.50 minutes a mile.

I passed a few interesting bands and singers that were perched on street corners, or outside old shops or launderettes. I think it's probably pretty unusual to see a live jazz band outside a launderette… and it was amazing how the music really picked me up. I felt like the band were playing for me alone and nobody else could hear them.

I took some Gatorade onboard at mile seven, knocking out eight minute miles at this stage, feeling good and pleased with my performance.

I was nearing the end of the long straight part of the race that I had spotted three miles earlier. The temperature had increased to eleven degrees now and I was very pleased with my body temperature, not overheating as I could still feel the chill in the air when I ran in the shade.

Something I found really strange was that I felt like I was passing lots of fellow runners, but not many seemed to be passing me. This meant one of two things: either I was going too fast and I would burn out or everybody I'd passed so far had gone off too fast and I was pacing myself correctly. I desperately hoped it was the latter.

Fortunately, as each mile passed and I still felt strong and confident it became more and more apparent that my pace was just as it should be.

At mile nine I was averaging 8.27 minutes a mile. I passed an R&B group rapping on the street. The rapper was dressed in a bright red jacket and perhaps the biggest and lowest hung jeans I'd ever seen. The bass line was going "Duff, duff" through me, the hairs on the back of my neck were standing up, runners were slowing down to start jumping and dancing, and I experienced a simply astonishing feeling as I ran through the streets of Brooklyn.

At this stage of a training run, I would have completed one of my regular routes. I knew how I should be feeling... and that was exactly how I was feeling right now. My increased training intensity over the last six weeks was really showing through today. All that hill training twice a week for four weeks - where I would run up a fairly steep gradient for four hundred metres, reach the top and then run a mid to fast pace back down and then repeat this up to four times - this had strengthened my quads so much and improved my heart rate performance, making it easier for me to run up the large bridges I was encountering here in New York.

I turned right up a fairly narrow street, a lovely tree-lined road with crowds of people on either side. I thought I must be in the Jewish quarter of Williamsburg as I spotted a large number of orthodox Jewish folk who seemed completely unaware that a major race was taking place. Two of the men, dressed in their black smock type coats and black trousers, walked straight out in front of me and I had to quickly adjust my pace to avoid a collision. It was as though they were running late for an appointment and were unaware that 47,000 runners were in their neighbourhood.

I reached the brow of the hill and as I looked down I could see about two miles in front of me again. It was exhilarating to see so much of the route ahead and it filled me with energy. My body felt right, no aches or pains at this stage, my time was good, and my watch continued to bleep 'slow down' across its screen. That meant I was running each mile in faster than eight minutes, which was my target, but I was also aware of going too fast too soon, and the watch kept my speed in check.

At mile 12 my time was one hour and thirty-seven minutes. This was great; I was on track to hit the half way point of 13.1 miles at around an hour and forty-six minutes. That would be really perfect, the ideal pace. I kept my concentration going, running a mental checklist at each mile that I passed. Legs ok? Knees? Back, feet, chest, temperature, thirst, hunger..,

As I went through the checklist I would tick each area as 'good', except that right now I was feeling a few hunger pains in the pit of my stomach. I ripped a Carbo Gel from my shorts. I put one end of the orange and silver packet between my teeth, ripped the end of the foil wrapper off and swallowed the contents just as I was approaching mile 13. I checked my watch and it bleeped at one hour forty-five minutes, Great! I took some water to digest the Carbo Gel as quickly as possible, almost visualising it fuelling my muscles and seeing me through the next seven miles.

The paper cups at the drinks stations were starting to annoy me; I was spilling as much as I was drinking. Maybe that was actually a good thing so I didn't take on too much water. Now, as good as I felt, I really did need these Carbo Gels. I broke the distance down and related it to my training distances of around nine miles, four miles, seven miles and six miles; my training milestones in distances that would hopefully see me through to a successful New York marathon.

My new mate Kevin had earlier commented on the number of bridges and steep inclines. So far I had completed two steep climbs, and then as I passed the half way stage of 13.1 miles I hit my third steep climb, a long winding approach to another bridge followed by a gentle downward run into the borough of Queens. I saw some spectators' signs saying "Welcome to Queens" along with other signs saying "Get out of Queens". it was nice to see that the locals had gone to such effort creating some light-hearted signs for the runners on entering and exiting the borough of Queens

I passed more runners, again noting that not many were passing me at mile 14...

I opted for Gatorade at the next drink station, the bright green sports drink splashing over my face, but I managed enough sips to quench my thirst.

I continued through the streets of New York and passed and acknowledged several bands, including a band playing disco music. The song playing as I pounded past was Sister Sledge's *We Are Family*. I felt like I was dancing in a nightclub. I looked to the sky and began singing for a few steps. Why does music make you feel so good, especially when you are running? It was an absolutely amazing feeling.

I passed through mile 15 at a pace of 8.45 minutes a mile. I was taking on more water this time as I was getting hotter, but thankfully not to the point of overheating like I had in the London Marathon. Or perhaps I knew what was waiting for me at mile 16... The massive Queensboro Bridge that links Queens to Manhattan. This is the stage of the race where the crowds are really noisy and enthusiastic. I would find out just how noisy and enthusiastic in the next few minutes.

I caught sight of the Queensboro Bridge and saw the approach; it looked menacing, with a large steep incline. I was still performing my frequent body checks after every mile and everything checked out as 'good', even my legs got the green light. In my previous marathons it was around this time that I started to tire, eventually hitting the wall at around seventeen or eighteen miles. So now was a crucial time, and I decided it was now or never for me to make best use my four weeks of hill training.

Woooooooshhhh... I climbed the hill onto the enclosed Queensboro Bridge, and it felt good. A few runners were slowing down or walking. Now, at such a crucial stage of the race, was not the time to walk. Never walk up a hill, I told myself, it's always twice as hard to get going again on a hill. I dug deep and read a fellow runner's t-shirt that said "I slept yesterday, I ran on Sunday, I drank on Sunday night". I kept reading those three lines over and over in my head to keep my mind from dwelling on how difficult this part of the race actually was.

As I passed this runner, I turned and told him what a great T-shirt he was wearing – that those inspirational words had really helped me up the hill and pretty much summed up how I was feeling. I started to think about the cold beer I would be having later in a bar in Greenwich, a cold beer in an ice cold glass. I could nearly taste it.

I continued onto the flat of Queenboro Bridge, voices and the sound of feet hitting tarmac echoing for the next five to ten minutes. I once again got myself back into the zone by following a slim, tanned looking female runner who looked South American. She was running the exact same pace as me, and that helped me focus again. I was locked into my zone until I reached the other side of the bridge where again there was daylight and sunshine. I could hear and then see the famously vocal masses cheering, screaming, shouting and ringing cow bells. The atmosphere was electric.

I had finally reached Manhattan at mile 16.

Back at the hotel, my wife Lucy had been meeting the wives and girlfriends of the Sports International runners to come along and watch; she'd said that she would aim to be at mile 16 to cheer me on. I searched and scanned everybody in the crowd, but couldn't see her. She would have seen me, surely? Or perhaps not. With most of my mind focused on the run it would have been easier for Lucy to spot me than me her, but there were no shouts of my name, and I continued onto 1st Avenue, heading northwards to the Bronx.

The sun was shining brightly, the roads were wide and busy with an even spread of runners everywhere and enough room for me to get to my next milestone of twenty miles without having to weave in and out of runners.

As I was nearing the Bronx I spotted a few spectator signs saying "Be careful in the Bronx" and "Run fast in the Bronx, you're gonna need to". I laughed to myself, briefly pondering the question 'Nobody's ever been attacked while running a New York marathon, have they?' Well, it certainly spurred me on; I was now ready to see what the Bronx was really like.

I passed mile 18 in two hours twenty minutes and decided to prepare my hydration tablet at mile 19. I was hoping this hydration tablet would prevent me from hitting the wall or cramping up in my thighs.

I had a challenge on my hands as I had to take the tablet from my plastic container inside the pocket of my shorts while running, drop it into the cup of water, run with it until it had dissolved, and then finally drink the resulting hydration drink without spilling any. It was a paper cup I was dealing with here, so I had to think of a solution that would work for me without stopping.

I thought about my IT job, where I was paid for providing solutions to my customer. This time I was the customer, so here goes. I reached mile 18 and slowed down to take the water. I then dropped the hydration tablet in, being careful not to spill anything. I then ran for another two minutes before sipping on the drink and feeling the nutrients of the tablet hit my body almost immediately. Still my main focus was not to spill any. I continued running very steadily until I arrived at the next water station at mile 19, and poured more water in.

I continued sipping away on my sports drink to hydrate myself fully with nearly a pint of hydration fluids. I continued slowly, ensuring I didn't spill any, and I felt I was tiring a little. It might just be because I was running through a boring and quiet industrial area on 1st Avenue, but a check of my watch revealed that my pace had dropped to 9.15 minutes a mile.

I reached the twenty mile mark at a steady pace of 9.30 minutes a mile. This was my third milestone in relation to my training runs. That's 75% of the race completed, I was thinking, it's time to dig even deeper and push myself. But don't go too quick, if anything keep the pace at 9.30 for the next few miles if need be. I knew I wanted a finish of anything under four hours and nine minutes a mile would clock a three hour fifty-six finish. I knew I was ahead of this at this stage, so things were looking good.

But this was a crucial point of the race. It could go either way. I knew I had to make the right decisions if I was going to succeed in my sub four-hour finish.

Before I knew it I was crossing another bridge, the rather flatter Willis Avenue Bridge, and then found myself in the Bronx.

I saw my first signs saying "Get out of the Bronx now!!", and "You're not welcome". My time at twenty miles was two hours fifty-four, bang on track. I continued to calculate the remaining miles in my head to pass the time, working out my potential finish time - and the race had gone exactly to plan up till this point.

I had memorised much of the route, so I knew that when I reached twenty-one miles I would be over my last bridge and back in Manhattan, and that the end was in sight. Well, I'd be in the last borough anyway.

As I plodded through the Bronx at a pace of 10.30 minutes a mile I slowed even more to allow two old American ladies to cross the road in front of me. It was like they were on a Sunday afternoon stroll, chatting to each other and waving their arms about to illustrate some trivial story, totally unaware that the runners were going past them.

I had reached my latest milestone of twenty-one miles, and had only five miles to go. I mean, anybody can run five miles, surely? I kept repeating that to myself and imagining me on my five-mile training run. As I left that final bridge I said goodbye to the Bronx, although I have to say, to my untrained eye the Bronx looked very similar to Queens and Brooklyn in terms of architecture. Had I not studied the route I'd have had no obvious indication that I'd left the borough.

I turned a sharp left onto 138th Street on the outskirts of Harlem and headed south onto the infamous 5th Avenue. This part of 5th Avenue was not the part that you would see in the big blockbuster films usually. I glanced around me and took in the sights of Harlem. It was a very old fashioned borough, almost like time had stood still for thirty years. It was something from a 1970s Starsky and Hutch episode, and it had a real slow pace about it, the people, and the vibe of the atmosphere. As I continued along 5th Avenue I could hear lots of singing and joyful music. I slowed down yet again, not only because it was an incredible gospel choir, but because I could suddenly feel a tiredness in my thighs. Thankfully it was uncomfortable rather than outright painful.

To distract myself, I concentrated on the gospel choir in their red robes with bright yellow trim. They were belting out the gospel anthem *O Happy Day*, and it was so impassioned it nearly brought a tear to my eye, although at this stage I wasn't sure if it was more down to the pain in my thighs.

I did my regular checks on the body and it seemed my hydration tablet, taken at the start and then at miles 18 and 19 had kept me from hitting the wall. I kept thinking that it could yet happen, although if I could get through the next couple of miles, I'd finish with a decent time, even under four hours... At twenty miles I'd been on track to achieve this. My friends, family and work colleagues were aware of the time I was looking at, as I had told my story of wanting to get into the sub four-hour club so many times and to so many people. I just didn't want to get carried away now as I was so close to the end.

I passed through mile 22 at a pace of 8.38 min/mile and took another water stop. The gradient of 5th Avenue at this stage was just a gentle incline, but it seemed to be taking its toll. I can't stop now, I thought, as soon as I did I would be struggling for the remainder of the race. The fact is that it's so much harder to start after stopping or walking during a marathon, as the muscles become tight as soon as you stop running.

Once again I went through my body checklist: legs, knees, back, body temperature, food. I felt hunger in my stomach again, so I ripped my third Carbo Gel open with my teeth to see me through the last few miles. Ahead and to either side of me I began to see casualties, people stopping with injuries or just plain exhaustion.

The gentle two-mile slope was taking its toll on me. This was the toughest part of the race and I felt drained, totally drained. My thighs were burning and with each step I took the pain was increasing. I had to make a firm decision not to stop, but to run through the pain barrier. Perhaps I needed more fluids to digest the Carbo Gel, or maybe I was hitting the wall - a very late wall. Or was it just a really tough part of the course? The muscles at the top of my legs were now aching, a low dull pain making me uncomfortable. Should I stop and walk now, perhaps not make the four-hour mark? Or should I just push myself one last bit and celebrate in style?

The crowds at this point were so noisy and there was music everywhere and the flags of various countries being waved. I spotted a British Union Jack flag and ran past a group of five British supporters. I exchanged a high five with them all, and with that I received a massive boost to keep me going.

I have never performed that well on hills, but boosted by my recent hill training I knew I had nearly reached the end…and then STOP!.

I had to stop and walk as the steady incline had got the better of me… I thought 'No! No!...'

I dug deep, counted thirty seconds a couple of times in my head and shouted 'Go! Go!' in my head...

Only a couple of miles to go through a lovely leafy park with lots of trees, meandering paths and greenery, over a few gentle rolling hills and that was it…Not too bad hey? NOT…

I had lots of these conversations in my head. How would it be if I told my story to my friends, family and work colleagues that I ran a perfect race for 22.5 miles… and then gave up?

Whhhhhoooooooossssshhhhhhhhhhhhhhhh!

I was off again, a slower pace of 10.5 min/mile just so I could get to the top of 5th Avenue before turning into Central Park. I looked ahead and saw runners doing exactly that; soon I could finally leave this two-mile stretch of pain, surely the hardest two miles I have ever completed.

24 – The Final Stages – Central Park

I turned right through the iron gates of Central Park, and felt that sense of honour to be here once again. It was like Hyde Park in London, lots of winding roads and gentle slopes going up and down.

I felt like I was over the worst of it now. I passed the twenty-four mile mark with a pace of 10.02 min/mile, and at the drinks station necked a Gatorade this time to mix it up a bit. I started to feel a lot stronger now for some reason, probably from the Carbo Gel , more fluids and not being on that terrible two-mile stretch of 5th Avenue.

I was on the flat again. I glanced at my watch for the 5000th time, checking my elapsed time, and current pace. The watch started to bleep to advise me that I was running a good pace again. Where had this energy reserve come from? I really couldn't explain it, but right now I felt how I'd felt at miles 9 and 10.

I started passing a few runners again, there were more and more injured runners along the way and I didn't want to be one of them now…NO WAY!

I was smiling inside by now, with a huge feeling of excitement about to explode in less than two miles. I followed the paths right, then left, then up and down until I saw the twenty-five mile point at 08.38 min/mile. There'd been moments when I didn't think that this sign would ever appear. One more water and an extra Gatorade this time.

I decided to run a little faster now as I was drank, having mastered the art of drinking from a paper cup on the run. I found I was near the exit of Central Park and back onto 5th Avenue again… not that dreadful 5th Avenue again.

I took a sharp right and came to the corner of Central Park and 5th Avenue where I knew the Plaza hotel is situated.

It was at this point that Lucy had said she would also be looking out for me, and I picked up my pace as I hoped that Lucy may be watching and shouting my name.

I was really missing her now and thinking about meeting up after the race and celebrating tonight. I would see her in a few minutes anyway or so I thought. As I ran along the south end of Central Park past the exclusive hotels, I saw yet another group of Union Jack flags. I moved across to the left of the street and swapped some more high fives just to keep me going for the last mile...

With under one mile to go I increased my pace again to 8.00 min/mile as I returned back into Central Park after passing by the famous Trump hotel. All of those rich and famous people watching me run the marathon, I thought... Or maybe not. Perhaps they would be drinking champagne and eating caviar instead...

In the distance I could make out the bright orange ING-sponsored finishing arch and lots of straw bales either side of the finishing straight.

The music was pumping and I picked my pace up yet again. The crowds were cheering every runner on, and I thought I was at Olympic pace now as I made my way towards the finish line as quick as I could.

Every second counts, a minute lost here and there...

I passed a few more runners, looked around left and right and then upward to the cameras and raised my arms aloft for the photographers to snap away at the closing moments of my first ever New York City Marathon...

"Yes!" I shouted…along with a few choice swear words of exhaustion…I put my finger on the stop of my watch - STOP!

I had done it…

I turned and shook the hands of various runners – people I had never seen in my life. I was filled with sheer jubilation that I had done it, and in the background the marathon officials were congratulating runners with "Good job" and "Hey you guys, great race."

I checked my watch.

My final time was an amazing three hours, forty-two minutes and twenty-one seconds…

3 hours,42 minutes,21 seconds.

Oh my word, I had smashed it! I'd wanted four hours but managed a massive eighteen minutes quicker…

I have never been so ecstatic in my life. I beat my best London Marathon time by twenty-three minutes. I felt on top of the world and I had a lump in my throat; in fact a tear ran down my face as I thought of everybody that knew me and how much this meant to me and of how the hard work I had put in had finally paid off. To this day I cannot decribe the elation of the race and how I felt. This will remain a special memory I shall treasure the rest of my life. Some people will compare it to seeing their newborn baby for the first time, and I'd find it hard to disagree.

25 – The Finish

"Keep walking", "Keep moving," the officials kept reminding the runners to move along the narrow paths of Central Park.

I walked past the two officials with large boxes of finishers' medals and was presented with my gold medal. I placed it around my neck and smiled.

As tired as I was, I continued walking and received a bright orange goodie bag a little further along the narrow path. I searched through the bag for food and drinks. I ate the mixed nuts, the breakfast bar, the apple and drank the water.

My legs now felt really sore and painful. I had hit the wall after the race had finished; a very odd feeling, but at least I had finished. I hobbled along awkwardly to the officials who were handing out the silver foil wraps to keep warm. I wrapped mine around me, but every time the wind blew my wrap would flap open. The sun was going down and could not find its way through the trees in the park, so the temperature was dropping. I could feel the autumn chill in the air now that I had stopped running.

I stopped walking with the crowds and moved to one side to perform a few muscular stretches so I didn't end up with cramp and unable to walk. Again I exchanged a few handshakes with fellow runners while stretching. I wanted to tell everybody that this was my PB, my best ever time in all three marathons. I was a novice really, but wanted to tell them how I conquered my ambition of running a marathon in under four hours, all while living and working a normal life. I was also a late starter to marathon running, with my first training starting in October 2008 at the age of 38.

I hobbled along the narrow pathways, being encouraged by the officials by saying what great race we had all run, and they were right. My legs were starting to seize up so I took another hydration tablet to ease the cramping in my thighs. I kept walking just to stay mobile enough to reach the UPS trucks where I could retrieve my belongings. It seemed like I was walking for an eternity, and it felt like I was back in Harlem again at the north end of Central Park.

As I caught sight of the UPS trucks I wondered if Lucy had seen me. I wonder if anybody knew my time. I was wondering all sorts of things as my mind raced away with so much excitement, so many stories to tell, so many amazing memories. I thought "Shall I stop running marathons now that I have reached my goal? Was this the end for me? Should I retire?"

I located my UPS truck and collected my clothing bag, accompanied by the hubbub of marathon officials being so complimentary, warm and friendly to every runner they encountered.

I stood to one side and dug deep in my bag to reach for my mobile and switched it on. There was very little network signal in the park, and my first attempt to call Lucy failed. I tried to send her a text message, but it simply wouldn't send. I tried to call her again, this time picking up a signal but being sent went straight to voicemail. I left a strange message, I think because my emotional state was so charged, and I wanted to hear Lucy's voice rather than a voicemail. I felt alone, but I wanted to let everybody know that I had triumphed in New York.

Lucy and I had a contingency plan to meet back at the hotel at three if we were unable to meet up after the race. Since this looked to be the case, I asked a marathon official the best way to exit Central Park. I left the park with my medal around my neck and my orange goodie bag and UPS clothing bag, still hobbling along, although the latest hydration tablet had reduced the pain somewhat and I felt a little easier.

I was at exit 81 in Central Park, looking for an easy route back to Times Square. I asked an official, who advised I should either take the subway or a taxi, about a hundred yards away at the end of the street, although I was still unsure of where I was. This may sound strange to some readers, but Central Park is nearly three miles long and I thought I was somewhere near the north end, in Harlem probably.

At last a block number: I was at 91st Street and my hotel was on 45th Street. I looked around to see chaos, traffic at a standstill, horns being sounded, people, orange bags and silver foils everywhere. Some runners looked like they had finished hours ago, and some had…

No chance of a taxi, so I glanced around and flagged down a cyclo - a bicycle with a double seat with a hood behind the cyclist. I asked the price to 45th Street and an eastern European-sounding accent replied "Twenty-five." "Twenty-five dollars?" I asked, and he kept nodding, So I climbed onto the cyclo and we were off ,zigzagging through the traffic, sometimes on the wrong side of the street and facing oncoming cars; quite an experience! I sat back and decided to call Lucy again. It just rang and rang, so I decided to leave a message, this time explaining my amazing time of three hours forty-two minutes and twenty-one seconds and the fact I was travelling back to the hotel on a cyclo - how funny is that? - and to meet me outside the hotel in fifteen minutes.

I held on and sat back to enjoy the ride. The wind was getting stronger as we headed south past Columbus Circle, so I put my layers of clothing back on as I sat on the fur-lined double seat of the cyclo. People were waving at me… did it look really strange with me sitting there and a medal hanging around my neck? Did I look like something from *Chariots of Fire*? It was very cold now, much like nine hours earlier when I'd first left the hotel.

As we approached Times Square, the cyclo driver pulled up at 47th Street as it would be quicker than going right to 45th Street. As I thanked him and stepped off the cyclo, he said "Ninety dollars."

I replied "How much?" in shock.

"Ninety dollars."

I told him it would be cheaper by taxi, to which he replied "We have travelled fifty blocks... Ok, that's sixty dollars."

I asked him why he'd kept saying twenty-five earlier, and his English accent suddenly improved as he explained that twenty-five blocks was forty-five dollars.

I said "There is no way I am paying that price, just because you think I am a tourist" and gave him forty dollars - which was still very expensive, twenty-eight British pounds - and told him what do to with his prices. As I hobbled across Times Square, he mumbled something unintelligible in his eastern European accent. I turned round and looked back at the expensive taxi ride, thinking it only costs fifty dollars from Times Square to JFK Airport in Queens, an hour's drive in an air-conditioned cab...

I really made a bad decision there, but I'd just wanted to be home.. On the plus side, it was my first bad decision that day.

I walked awkwardly up two blocks and arrived at the Marriott Marquis hotel. I passed through the revolving door, looking out for Lucy, pressed the button for the elevator to go to the 33rd floor and before I knew it the doors had opened. Just a few more steps until I was back in the hotel room where I could finally rest.

I opened the hotel room door expecting Lucy to greet me and she wasn't there. I still couldn't share my success story and elation with anybody.

Suddenly my mobile phone bleeped. It was a text message from Lucy congratulating me on my amazing race time. She had been watching the race with the wives and girlfriends of the runners from Sports International and had been waiting at mile 25 next to the Plaza hotel, but didn't see me. She was on her way back to the hotel and would be with me in twenty minutes...

I was relieved that I had heard Lucy's voice and that at last I could share my story with somebody in detail. I was bursting with excitement to talk about my amazing experience.

I sat down on the sofa and just stopped. I stretched out on the big comfy cushioned sofa for around five minutes in silence ,taking in what I had achieved today and reliving some of the moments of the eight hours since I'd left Lucy that morning. It was now three o'clock and I continued in silence, closed my eyes, not to sleep, but just to empty my buzzing head and return to stillness.,

Finally I opened my eyes and pulled the blinds back and watched the busy Times Square activities, still in restful silence. I cherished this five minutes, and my mind turned to my colleague Brian and his misfortune in missing out on this mind-blowing experience., all because of a sickness bug.

Click.

The hotel door opened to reveal Lucy with perhaps the biggest smile I'd seen on her face. She came rushing up to me, kissed , hugged and congratulated me. I felt very special, but felt even better when she produced a bottle of chilled champagne from her shopping bag...WOW!

We swapped stories about how we'd missed each other at mile 16 and then again at mile 25, and then with the text message failure and failed phone call. We were so glad to be reunited again.

We agreed that Sunday would be the first real night out, as I had been eating and drinking so healthily for the previous two nights. But tonight was the night to celebrate. We sipped the champagne, and I could feel the bubbles going to my head very quickly. Most fitness books you read tell you not to drink alcohol so soon after a race, but I had finished over an hour ago, had been eating and drinking to replenish my body and was feeling pretty good even before the bubbles. It felt great that my 'alcohol ban' had been lifted, even if it hadn't been a blanket ban.

We chatted about the sights and how I felt at each stage of the race; we discussed where Lucy was standing during the race and how we hadn't see each other, which was, I suppose, hardly surprising with 47,000 runners. Lucy had made some nice new friends among the wives and girlfriends of the Sports International group runners, people who knew what it was like to listen, breathe and sleep PB talk, in fact marathon *anything..*

The 9 – 5 Marathon Man

This picture shows the marathon masses at the start of the New York City Marathon on the Verrazano-Narrows Bridge

View of Staten Island at the Green Start Area

This picture show the masses at the 10k point in Brooklyn, running the wide streets for about 8 miles

This picture above shows the half way stage at 13.1 miles on the approach to yet another bridge.

The final stages at mile 23 in Central Park, tired and on my last legs, looking for inspiration.

The final stages at mile 25, just before entering Central Park for the last time.

The closing stages of the race, the last few yards before finishing in 3 hours, 42 minutes and 21 seconds

The finish line… at last

26 – Celebrations in Greenwich Village

It was just after half four and the sun had set and it looked freezing outside. I had a relaxing bath to soothe my tired body, although I was relieved to note that I didn't feel too bad compared to previous marathons, so I'd expected to feel a lot worse. As I climbed out of the bath I could feel a stiffness in the tops of my legs - my quads going down to my knees - but that was it. Frankly I felt lucky to only be *this* sore.

We were ready to leave the hotel by 18:00 to hit the bright lights of New York. We were off to Greenwich Village to celebrate my marathon success. The taxi queues were very long at the hotel, so we walked onto Broadway to hail a taxi. We waited and waited, eventually heading to a nearby hotel queue at the taxi rank. Still no sign of an available taxi, probably due to the marathon; a bit of a knock-on effect. So we decided to take the subway, our first trip on the subway for many years.

We went down the steps on 47th Street, hoping to go on the red line southbound to Franklin Street, but the ticket office was closed, I had no loose change, the change machine was broken and out of order, and there was nobody to ask except a foreign cleaner who I wasn't convinced understood me; he just informed me that I had to take the first train somewhere, then change and take a particular number train…at which point we became too confused. this appeared very confusing.

I just wanted to celebrate now! I wanted to be in a New York jazz bar and have a few well deserved beers with dinner and spend the night with Lucy, relaxing…

We walked back up to ground level again, where our second attempt to get a taxi failed. My mood was changing, my body was giving signs that it was going to hurt and ache if a solution was not found very soon and above all I just wanted a beer!

After all that had happened to me today I guess my luck had to turn at some point.

We decided to walk to 42nd Street , where we went down to the subway again, bought a ticket, found the correct train and took the slow southbound train heading for South Ferry. Six stops later we jumped off at Franklin Street. It wasn't that difficult really was it? I think my emotions were just frayed and raw, and I was physically and mentally pretty drained.

We reached street level of Franklin Street at last. It was dark and very quiet, a few dingy lights in one direction, a few empty restaurants in another. We had five roads to choose from…which should we take? We went for the road that looked the liveliest. Unfortunately we couldn't find the particular jazz bar we'd spotted earlier in the New York guide books and agreed that the next bar we stumbled across we would just go into for a beer and chill out!

We stumbled across a typical American bar on a street corner, walked in and immediately liked the buzzing atmosphere. It was so busy, with lots of laughing and joking and music on in the background. Lucy found us a nice table with high stools in the window. I went to the bar and ordered a premium Belgian beer - a strong start to my night - and a large Sauvignon Blanc from New Zealand for Lucy… Gulp, gulp… I loved every sip of that perfectly chilled Belgian beer.

Everywhere I looked in the bar I could see fellow marathon runners wearing the finisher's medal; I was amused to see that the locals seemed to be so proud to be wearing them.

I finished my first beer in less than ten minutes; it slipped down my throat all the more smoothly after not drinking beer for nearly 6 weeks. I ordered another while Lucy was slowly sipping her wine, and the barman seemed quite shocked that I'd asked for another in such a short space of time.

We glanced around the bar, packed with excited but tired post-marathon revellers who must surely be feeling exactly as I did. I was on such a high and sharing my stories again with Lucy. She had to be a good listener after I'd talked continuously for over an hour about the day's events. As time ticked by we ordered food and a bottle of wine, and I was buzzing and ready for a big night out. I sipped away, glass after glass of wine, and our food could not arrive quick enough. After three Belgian beers and nearly a half bottle of wine my vision was becoming a little blurred...

I went to jump down from my high stool, and not only were the tops of my legs sore, but my right leg gave way completely and I fell to the floor. It was conceivable that the alcohol taking its toll now... Lucy just laughed at me, while I staggered off to the toilets and tripped on a concrete step along the way. Even so, I just had a permanent smile on my face after what I had achieved today. I didn't have a care in the world right now.

We finished the bottle of wine and then had a couple more drinks to finish; in fact to finish us both off. We settled the bill and exchanged a few words with the barman. He simply smiled at us, so I ended up telling him the day's events as If I was the only person in New York to have run the marathon. Thankfully, he humoured me.

We left the bar a few minutes later and staggered outside to hail a taxi to the hotel. I flagged a taxi down, we jumped in and took the short ride up 9th Avenue to Broadway and 45th Street, followed by a quick ride in the elevator to our room.

I closed the door behind us and checked my watch. It was very blurred and it read 21:20, Sunday 6th November. We were back so early...

It'll come as no surprise that I slept well.

27 – Monday 7th November, the Day After

I woke up at seven and checked every part of my body to see which parts were painful. The top of my legs and my thighs were still very sore, but no worse than yesterday. I eased myself out of bed, feeling hungry. I just had to eat, although it felt like I hadn't stopped eating for twenty-four hours. Oddly, in previous marathons I'd actually gone off my food. My morning routine each day in New York was two cups of English breakfast tea and a cereal bar, and today was no different.

Lucy and I left the hotel at half eight, heading to Wall Street on the subway to take a look around the Ground Zero memorial site. It was today that we were starting the relaxing part of the trip to New York... Ahhh, relax...

It was another cold but very sunny day, which we were told was very unusual for this time of the year. We took the subway on the red line again on 42nd Street and went south to Wall Street subway station. During the twenty-minute journey I must have seen thirty or forty people wearing the marathon finisher's medal around their neck, and even wearing the ING 2011 official marathon clothing. I found this a bit strange to begin with, but when people could still be seen wearing them later in the day in the bars of the West Village, Tribeca and the Meatpacking District and even the day after, on Tuesday on 5th Avenue, I began to find it downright annoying.

As each day passed I saw this less and less as the runners from around the world were departing. On Thursday 9th November Lucy and I departed New York at seven thirty in the evening, thoroughly satisfied with a successful and exciting trip to New York for the marathon.

The Virgin Atlantic plane touched down at Heathrow on Friday 10th November, a cold and foggy return to reality. I was back to work before I knew it, work colleagues congratulating me and asking about the trip, followed by a long chat with Brian where I shared my amazing experiences of the trip to New York and running the marathon.

28 – How Did I Achieve My Goal?

As the plane took off I sat in my seat and reflected on my dream in New York.

From the moment we'd landed in New York the previous week, in my heart I'd known it was going to be an amazing week and I'd known I was going to run the marathon in under four hours.

I was immensely proud of what I'd achieved, following two London Marathons of four hours fifteen and four hours and five, and then that crushing blow to my 2011 London Marathon hopes

Now everybody knew how focused I was between April and New York, and that my training plan was very strict. But in fact I didn't start my training plan until mid-August. I'd trawled the internet so I could follow a pretty rigid marathon plan that would provide the assistance I needed to succeed.

I found Hal Higdon's training plan was perfect for me. Hal was long distance runner and running writer who clocked up 111 marathons. His plan was based over a seven-day period with one day of rest, although I myself quite often took two days off each week.

I found having a training plan incredibly useful. Each day I would check to see how many miles I would be running and what type of run it would be. The possibilities included fast, slow and fartlek, with distances ranging from four, six and eight miles during the week to the long runs on Sunday of ten, twelve, thirteen, sixteen, eighteen, twenty and twenty-two before tapering off in the last few weeks.

I kept to the schedule as much as possible, usually having my rest day the day after or the before the long run. This I believe to be one of the keys of my successful training. I had a plan that I stuck to.

I also think that you can follow any plan, but you also need the desire to succeed. In my case, after my back injury in April, I believed I could do virtually anything. That's the reason that on the flight to New York I knew – rather than hoped – that I could achieve my dream.

Along with the intensive training plan, I managed to get myself signed up for a couple of races - match practice if you will. I raced a half-marathon in Oxford in an hour and 42 minutes and then a 10K run on a very hot Sunday morning in 44 minutes. These races gave me a good gauge of my marathon pace in testing conditions.

My training runs were much quicker too, taking several minutes off each run. It was like I had learnt how to run correctly. Each run I completed I could predict my finish time down to the nearest few seconds, especially on my favourite 8.63 mile (1/3 of marathon distance). I calculated my potential marathon pace times on these runs, even though I knew that would be unrealistic. As an example, on the basis I completed a third of a marathon in one hour and seven minutes, I'd complete the full marathon in three hours twenty-one. Now of course I knew that was optimistic as I would drop my 7.40 min/mile pace as I reached miles 17, 18, and 19, before aiming to pick up towards the end. And that was exactly what happened in New York. I really felt I had understood my thresholds with pace and distance..

Perhaps it was the last few weeks of hill training which allowed me to score that target time. Twice a week I would run four laps of a steep hill for 300 metres without stopping, followed by a sprint down the hill and on the flat at a pace of 7.40 min/mile This was great cardio work for me, and it must surely have helped me over the many bridges in New York, some of which were so steep it was unreal that I could run up them at all, let alone run up them at pace.

Another secret was my watch. Initially I'd used my iPhone 4 and MapMyRUN app, but this meant I had to wear a runner's waist belt to carry the heavy phone. When I ran the Oxford Half-Marathon the penny finally dropped and I invested in the Garmin 305 GPS running watch. It told me everything and did everything, tracking my pace, distance, calories and split times, it issued pace alerts and saved the extra weight and niggling discomfort of the waistband and phone.

Finally my lifestyle was the final key to me succeeding and improving my fitness to a level where I could run a marathon comfortably. I cut out drinking beer from Sunday 2nd October, six weeks prior to New York. I was still drinking wine on a Saturday night, but only a two or three glasses. So my alcohol intake reduced dramatically in the last month and a half, virtually down to zero.

Each day I would eat cereal for breakfast, drink lots of water throughout the day, eat a healthy salad of around 300 calories, some mixed fruit and a banana before my evening run at 6.30pm. Our evening meal consisted of salads and meat, often chicken or vegetables, but simply cutting out chocolate, biscuits, takeaways and general junk. I only ate when I was hungry, and I only ate healthily.

So my areas of discovery that I would recommend 100% are as below:

- Marathon training plan
- Diet
- Low alcohol consumption, down to zero two weeks before
    - No beer for six weeks or more, and only the odd glass of wine
- Hill training

- Garmin 305 GPS running watch – or your own personal preference
- Competitive races.

My final thoughts are these: if you have a realistic goal, and you want it enough, you need to work hard for it. You'll have good days and bad days during the journey, and you'll need to be strict with your training even when you don't feel like it at all.

But to achieve anything you must first learn about yourself, understand your capabilities and limits and push yourself, keep motivated, shut out the work issues and any personal issues that you may have during training, and to try to surround yourself with supportive family and friends.

Anybody can succeed if they really want to. This is one of my biggest personal achievements in life, to run a marathon in less than four hours, to complete the New York City Marathon in three hours, forty-two minutes and twenty-one seconds is amazing... I smashed it.

My final word... four weeks after the New York City Marathon, Lucy found out she was pregnant with our first baby, an absolutely beautiful present for both of us.

The 9 – 5 Marathon Man

The 9 – 5 Marathon Man

The 9 – 5 Marathon Man

THE END